SOURCES FOR PATTERNS OF WORLD HISTORY

VOLUME ONE: TO 1600

SOURCES FOR PATTERNS OF WORLD HISTORY

VOLUME ONE: TO 1600

EDITED BY

Jonathan S. Perry

UNIVERSITY OF SOUTH FLORIDA, SARASOTA-MANATEE

NEW YORK OXFORD

OXFORD UNIVERSITY PRESS

Oxford University Press is a department of the University of Oxford. It furthers the University's objective of excellence in research, scholarship, and education by publishing worldwide.

Oxford New York
Auckland Cape Town Dar es Salaam Hong Kong Karachi
Kuala Lumpur Madrid Melbourne Mexico City Nairobi
New Delhi Shanghai Taipei Toronto

With offices in
Argentina Austria Brazil Chile Czech Republic France Greece
Guatemala Hungary Italy Japan Poland Portugal Singapore
South Korea Switzerland Thailand Turkey Ukraine Vietnam

For titles covered by Section 112 of the US Higher Education Opportunity Act, please visit www.oup.com/us/he for the latest information about pricing and alternate formats.

Published in the United States of America by
Oxford University Press
198 Madison Avenue, New York, NY 10016
http://www.oup.com

Library of Congress Cataloging-in-Publication Data
Sources in Patterns of world history / [edited by] Jonathan Perry. -- Second edition.
volumes cm
Summary: "A sourcebook of primary sources collected to complement OUP's textbook Patterns of World History, 2nd edition"--Provided by publisher.
Contents: Volume One. To 1600 -- Volume Two. Since 1400.
ISBN 978-0-19-939972-7 (volume 1 : paperback : acid-free paper) --
ISBN 978-0-19-939973-4 (volume 2 : paperback : acid-free paper) 1. World history--Sources.
I. Perry, Jonathan Scott. II. Von Sivers, Peter. Patterns of world history.
D21.S6755 2015
909--dc23

2014020327

Printing number: 9 8 7 6 5 4 3 2 1

Printed in the United States of America
on acid-free paper

CONTENTS

HOW TO READ A PRIMARY SOURCE

This sourcebook is composed of eighty-seven primary sources. A primary source is any text, image, or other source of information that gives us a first-hand account of the past by someone who witnessed or participated in the historical events in question. While such sources can provide significant and fascinating insight into the past, they must also be read carefully to limit modern assumptions about historical modes of thought. Here are a few elements to keep in mind when approaching a primary source.

AUTHORSHIP

Who produced this source of information? A male or a female? A member of the elite or of the lower class? An outsider looking *in* at an event or an insider looking *out*? What profession or lifestyle does the author pursue, which might influence how he is recording his information?

GENRE

What type of source are you examining? Different genres—categories of material—have different goals and stylistic elements. For example, a personal letter meant exclusively for the eyes of a distant cousin might include unveiled opinions and relatively trivial pieces of information, like the writer's vacation plans. On the other hand, a political speech intended to convince a nation of a leader's point of view might subdue personal opinions beneath artful rhetoric and focus on large issues like national welfare or war. Identifying genre can be useful for deducing how the source may have been received by an audience.

AUDIENCE

Who is reading, listening to, or observing the source? Is it a public or private audience? National or international? Religious or nonreligious? The source may be geared toward the expectations of a particular group; it may be recorded in a language that is specific to a particular group. Identifying audience can help us understand why the author chose a certain tone or why he included certain types of information.

HISTORICAL CONTEXT

When and why was this source produced? On what date? For what purposes? What historical moment does the source address? It is paramount that we approach primary sources in context to avoid anachronism (attributing an idea or habit to a past era where it does not belong) and faulty judgment. For example, when considering a medieval history, we must take account of the fact that in the Middle Ages, the widespread understanding was that God created the world and could still interfere in the activity of mankind—such as sending a terrible storm when a community had sinned. Knowing the context (Christian, medieval, views of the world) helps us to avoid importing modern assumptions—like the fact that storms are caused by atmospheric pressure—into historical texts. In this way we can read the source more faithfully, carefully, and generously.

BIAS AND FRAMING

Is there an overt argument being made by the source? Did the author have a particular agenda? Did any political or social motives underlie the reasons for writing the document? Does the document exhibit any qualities that offer clues about the author's intentions?

STYLISTIC ELEMENTS

Stylistic features such as tone, vocabulary, word choice, and the manner in which the material is organized and presented should also be considered when examining a source. They can provide insight into the writer's perspective and offer additional context for considering a source in its entirety.

SOURCES FOR PATTERNS OF WORLD HISTORY

VOLUME ONE: TO 1600

1. THE AFRICAN ORIGINS OF HUMANITY, PREHISTORY–10,000 BCE

1.1 Shell Bead Jewelry from the Grotte des Pigeons, Taforalt, Morocco, ca. 82,000–75,000 YBP

The discovery of 13 shells in a cave in eastern Morocco in 2007 has led to a discussion about the oldest known form of human ornamentation. Because each shell contains a pierced hole and traces of red ochre (a pigment derived from clay), archaeologists concluded that the shells had been strung together as necklaces or bracelets. Another important detail is that the shell is from a genus of marine snail called *Nassarius*. The closest this snail is found to the site (at least today) is an island off the coast of Tunisia, more than 800 miles away.

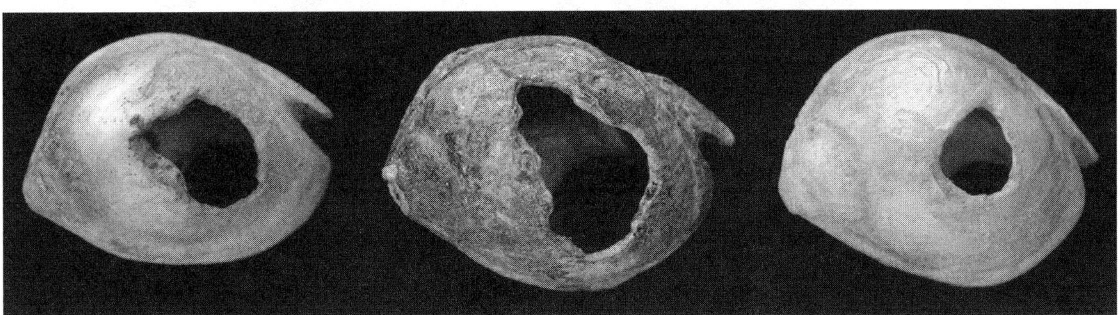

WORKING WITH SOURCES

1. Why is the creation of jewelry a significant step in the development of human society?
2. What might this find indicate about trade patterns and networks in northern Africa around 80,000 years ago?

YBP: Years Before Present.

Source: Smithsonian Institution, National Museum of Natural History, http://humanorigins.si.edu/category/tags/292

1.2 Python-Shaped Ornamented Rock Found in the Rhino Cave, Botswana, ca. 70,000 YBP

Archaeologists working in the Tsodilo Hills of Botswana in 2006 may have found the oldest evidence of a form of human ritual behavior. One cavern contains a large rock, roughly 20 feet long and 6.5 feet wide, that resembles a giant python, with the natural features of the stone forming its eye and mouth. While its resemblance to a reptile may be natural, there are also several hundred man-made grooves along its side, indicating an attempt to replicate scales with fashioned tools. Spearheads were also found at the site, and similar ones in the area have been dated to 77,000 years ago. Researchers have concluded that this was a worship site for the inhabitants of the region in this period.

WORKING WITH SOURCES

1. What symbolic connections might early humans have attributed to snakes, and why might snakes have been depicted and worshipped?
2. What does the growth of "abstract symbolic thinking" suggest about the development of early *H. sapiens* societies?

Source: National Geographic, http://news.nationalgeographic.com/news/2006/12/061222-python-ritual.html

1.3 Paintings in the Cave of Altamira, Santillana del Mar, Spain, ca. 22,000–14,000 YBP

Inspired by the excitement attending the discovery of prehistoric cave paintings in France, amateur Spanish archaeologist Marcelino Sanz de Sautuola (1831–1888) conducted work on a Spanish cave in which similar paintings had been found. A series of excavations have been undertaken in the years since, leading to the discovery of many objects made from **silex**, bone, and horn at various levels of the cave system. The paintings—of horses, deer, bison, and human hands—were made throughout the cave's occupation, and the images are generally outlined in a black charcoal pigment and filled in with red or yellow paint.

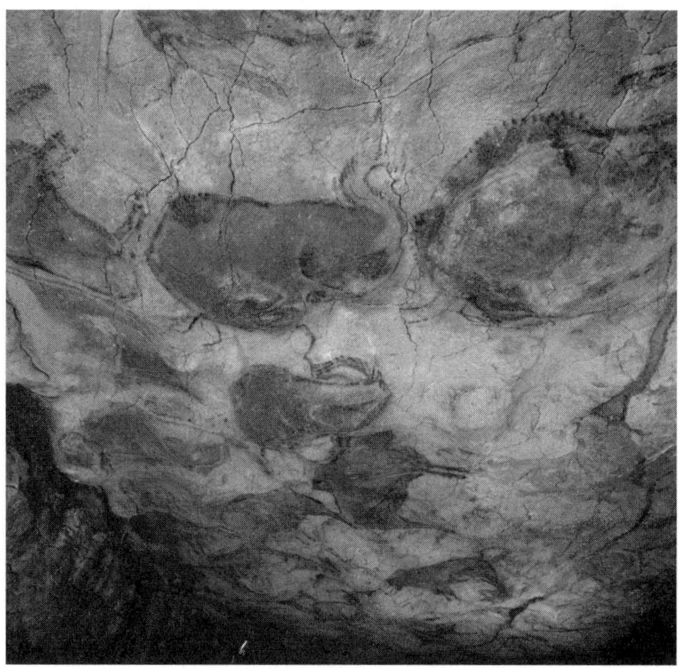

WORKING WITH SOURCES

1. What do these images depict, and how can they be compared with the paintings found at Lascaux and Trois-Frères, France?
2. What do the artistic and technical accomplishments of these artists indicate about the cultural creativity of early humans?

Silex: Finely-ground stone used as pigment in paint.

Source: Museo de Altamira, Spain, http://en.museodealtamira.mcu.es/Prehistoria_y_Arte/index.html

1.4 Flax Fibers Found at the Dzudzuana Cave, Republic of Georgia, Caucasus Mountains, ca. 30,000 YBP

A 2009 paper in *Science* announced the identification of at least 488 fibers of flax attached to clay samples found in a cave in Georgia, in the Caucasus. Some of these fibers had been spun and dyed, and one of the threads (no. 8 below) had been twisted. The applied colors, ranging from black to gray to turquoise, may indicate that the inhabitants of the cave were engaged in producing colorful textiles. The presence of spores in the cave indicates that fungus was probably already growing on the clothes and progressively breaking them down.

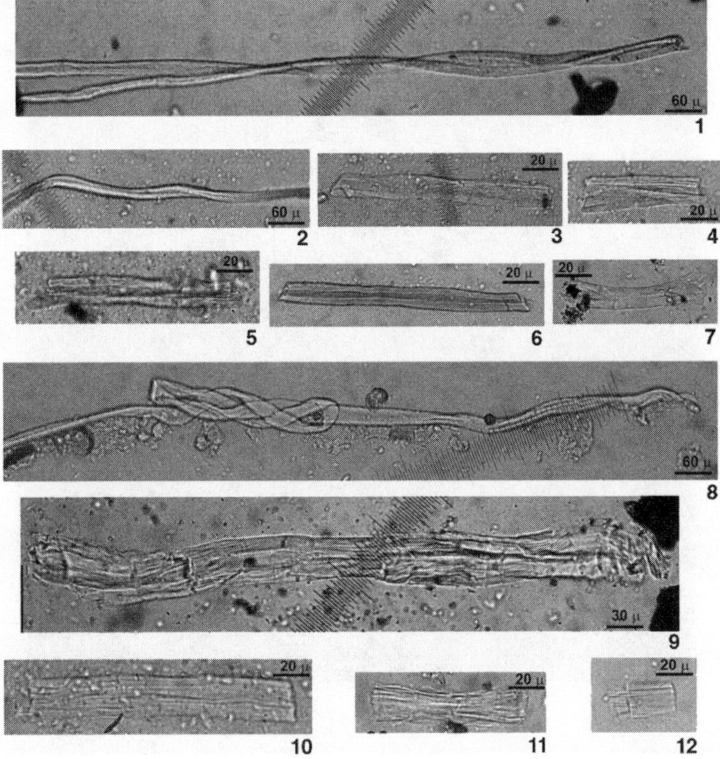

WORKING WITH SOURCES

1. What does the manufacture of clothing suggest about the sophistication of Upper Paleolithic human societies?
2. Can the manufacture of textiles in this period be compared to other forms of handcraft in the same era?

Source: Science Magazine, 11 September 2009, http://www.sciencemag.org/content/325/5946/1359.full#xref-ref-2-1

2. AGRARIAN–URBAN CENTERS OF THE MIDDLE EAST AND EASTERN MEDITERRANEAN, 11,500–600 BCE

2.1 Law Code of Hammurabi, ca. 1772 BCE

In order to "cause justice to prevail in the land" and to "further the welfare of the people," the Amorite King Hammurabi (ca. 1792–1750 BCE), having made Babylon his capital and having conquered Mesopotamia, issued a comprehensive code of laws. He caused them to be inscribed on stones that were erected at crossroads and in marketplaces throughout his kingdom, so that all his subjects would understand the penalties that their actions might incur. This document survives on one of these stones, topped by an illustration showing Hammurabi receiving the order to write as directed by the sun god Shamash. The stone was discovered by French archaeologists in 1901–1902, and it remains one of the treasures of the Louvre Museum in Paris.

1. If a man accuse a man, and charge him with murder, but cannot convict him, the accuser shall be put to death.

3. If a man in a case before the court offer testimony concerning deeds of violence, and do not establish the testimony he has given . . . the man shall be put to death.

53. If a man neglect to strengthen his dike, and do not strengthen his dike, and a break be made in his dike and he let the water carry away farmland, then the man in whose dike the break has been made shall restore the grain which he has damaged.

54. If he be not able to restore the grain, they shall sell him and his goods, and the farmers whose grain the water has carried away shall divide the results of the sale.

104. If a merchant give an agent grain, wood, oil, or goods of any kind with which to trade, the agent shall write down the money received and return it to the merchant. The agent shall take a sealed receipt for the money which he gives to the merchant.

105. If the agent be careless and do not take a receipt for the money which he has given to the merchant, the money not receipted for shall not be placed to his account.

196. If a man destroy the eye of another man, they shall destroy his eye.

197. If he break a man's bone, they shall break his bone.

Source: Nels M. Bailkey and Richard Lim, eds., *Readings in Ancient History: Thought and Experience from Gilgamesh to St. Augustine*, 6th ed. (Boston: Houghton Mifflin 2002), 28–36.

198. If he destroy the eye of a common man or break a bone of a common man, he shall pay one *mina* of silver.

199. If he destroy the eye of a man's slave or break a bone of a man's slave, he shall pay one-half his price.

206. If a man strike another man in a quarrel and wound him, that man shall swear, "I did not strike him intentionally," and he shall be responsible for the physician.

207. If he die as a result of the blow, he shall swear as above, and if it were the son of a gentleman, he shall pay one-third *mina* of silver.

228. If a builder erect a house for a man and complete it, he shall give him two shekels of silver per *sar* of house as his wage.

229. If a builder erect a house for a man and do not make its construction firm and the house which he built collapse and cause the death of the owner of the house, that builder shall be put to death.

233. If a builder erect a house for a man and do not surround it with walls of proper construction, and a wall fall in, that builder shall strengthen that wall at his own expense.

253. If a man hire a man to oversee his farm and furnish him the seed-grain and entrust him with oxen and contract with him to cultivate the field, and that man steal either the seed or the crop and it be found in his possession, they shall cut off his fingers.

From the Epilogue:
The great gods proclaimed me, and I am the guardian shepherd whose scepter is righteous and whose beneficent shadow is spread over my city. In my bosom I carried the people of the land of Sumer and Akkad; under my protection I brought their brethren into security; in my wisdom I sheltered them.

That the strong might not oppress the weak, and that they should give justice to the orphan and the widow. . . .

WORKING WITH SOURCES

1. When are financial and capital punishments applied in the code, and is there a consistent principle at work here?
2. Why is Hammurabi concerned with the regulation of business transactions, and particularly when they have to do with agriculture?

2.2 Babylonian Poem of the Righteous Sufferer, ca. 2000–1600 BCE

Composed in Akkadian and consisting of 480 lines distributed over four tablets, this poem is a protest against one man's undeserved suffering. The author is tormented but cannot determine the cause, and he feels that the god Marduk is not responding adequately to his lamentation.

Source: Nels M. Bailkey and Richard Lim, eds., *Readings in Ancient History: Thought and Experience from Gilgamesh to St. Augustine*, 6th ed. (Boston: Houghton Mifflin 2002), 20–22.

Because he has always been faithful to his god and assiduous in his worship, the Sufferer begins to speculate that the gods are not concerned with human pain at all. Even more, they may engage in this sort of torment for their own benefit. The figure of the "Righteous Sufferer" is frequently compared to the Biblical figure Job. While this "Babylonian Job" is eventually delivered from his sufferings, perhaps his complaints linger on.

My god has forsaken me and disappeared,
My goddess has failed me and keeps at a distance.
The benevolent angel who walked beside me has departed,
My protecting spirit has taken to flight, and is seeking someone else.
My strength is gone; my appearance has become gloomy;
My dignity has flown away, my protecting made off. . . .
The king, the flesh of the gods, the sun of his peoples,
His heart is enraged with me, and cannot be appeased.
The courtiers plot hostile action against me,
They assemble themselves and give utterance to impious words. . . .
They combine against me in slander and lies.
My lordly mouth have they held as with reins,
So that I, whose lips used to prate, have become like a mute.
My sonorous shout is reduced to silence,
My lofty head is bowed down to the ground,
Dread has enfeebled my robust heart. . . .
If I walk the street, ears are pricked;
If I enter the palace, eyes blink.
My city frowns on me as an enemy;
Indeed my land is savage and hostile.

. . .

My ill luck has increased, and I do not find the right.
I called to my god, but he did not show his face,
I prayed to my goddess, but she did not raise her head.
The diviner with his inspection has not got to the root of the matter,
Nor has the dream priest with his libation elucidated my case.
I sought the favor of the ***zaqiqu*-spirit**, but he did not enlighten me;
And the incantation priest with his ritual did not appease the divine wrath against me.
What strange conditions everywhere!
When I look behind, there is persecution, trouble.

. . .

For myself, I gave attention to supplication and prayer:
To me prayer was discretion, sacrifice my rule.
The day for reverencing the god was a joy to my heart;
The day of the goddess' procession was profit and gain to me.
The king's prayer—that was my joy,
And the accompanying music became a delight for me.
I instructed my land to keep the god's rites,
And provoked my people to value the goddess' name.
I made praise for the king like a god's
And taught the populace reverence for the palace.
I wish I knew that these things were pleasing to one's god!

What is proper to oneself is an offense to one's god,
What in one's heart seems despicable is proper to one's god.
Who knows the will of the gods in heaven?

***Zaqiqu*-spirit:** The god of dreams.

Who understands the plans of the underworld
gods?
Where have mortals learnt the way of a god?
He who was alive yesterday is dead today.
For a minute he was dejected, suddenly he is
exuberant.
One moment people are singing in exaltation,
Another they groan like professional mourners.

WORKING WITH SOURCES

1. What is the responsibility of the gods to this worshipper, and what can he do if the gods renege on the contract?
2. How are the priestly establishment and the king connected to this man? Have these institutions also failed him?

2.3 Advice from a Royal Scribe to His Apprentice, Middle Kingdom Egypt Twelfth Dynasty, ca. 1878–1839 BCE

The Papyrus Lansing is a letter of instruction from the royal scribe (and "chief overseer of the cattle of Amun-Re, King of Gods") Nebmare-nakht to his apprentice Wenemdiamun. It seems to date from the reign of the pharaoh Senusret III (Sesostris III). The letter conveys a great deal of practical advice to an up-and-coming scribe—as well as warnings about what temptations he must avoid to be successful. While Nebmare-nakht is clearly proud of the status his work has earned him, he also illuminates the specific duties and responsibilities of a royal official in this period.

The scribe of the army and commander of the cattle of the house of Amun, Nebmare-nakht, speaks to the scribe Wenemdiamun, as follows. Be a scribe! Your body will be sleek; your hand will be soft. You will not flicker like a flame, like one whose body is feeble. For there is not the bone of a man in you. You are tall and thin. If you lifted a load to carry it, you would stagger, your legs would tremble. You are lacking in strength; you are weak in all your limbs; you are poor in body.

Set your sight on being a scribe: a fine profession that suits you. You call for one; a thousand answer you. You stride freely on the road. You will not die like a hired ox. You are in front of others.

I spend the day instructing you. You do not listen! Your heart is like an empty room. My teachings are not in it. Take their meaning to yourself!

The marsh thicket is before you each day, as a nestling is after its mother. You follow the path of pleasure; you make friends with revelers. You have made your home in the brewery, as one who thirsts for beer. You sit in the parlor with an idler. You hold the writings in contempt. You visit the prostitute. Do not do these things! What are they for? They are of no use. Take note of it!

Furthermore. Look, I instruct you to make you sound; to make you hold the palette freely. To make you

Source: Translated by A. M. Blackman and T. E. Peet, *Journal of Egyptian Archaeology* 11 (1925): 284–298, as quoted by Miriam Lichtheim, *Ancient Egyptian Literature*, vol. 2 (Berkeley: University of California Press, 1978), 171–172.

become one whom the king trusts; to make you gain entrance to treasury and granary. To make you receive the ship-load at the gate of the granary. To make you issue the offerings on feast days. You are dressed in fine clothes; you own horses. Your boat is on the river; you are supplied with attendants. You stride about inspecting. A mansion is built in your town. You have a powerful office, given you by the king. Male and female slaves are about you. Those who are in the fields grasp your hand, on plots that you have made. Look, I make you into a staff of life! Put the writings in your heart, and you will be protected from all kinds of toil. You will become a worthy official.

Do you not recall the fate of the unskilled man? His name is not known. He is ever burdened [like an ass carrying] in front of the scribe who knows what he is about.

Come, let me tell you the woes of the soldier, and how many are his superiors: the general, the troop-commander, the officer who leads, the standard-bearer, the lieutenant, the scribe, the commander of fifty, and the garrison-captain. They go in and out in the halls of the palace, saying, "Get laborers!". . . .

His march is uphill through mountains. He drinks water every third day; it is smelly and tastes of salt. His body is ravaged by illness. The enemy comes, surrounds him with missiles, and life recedes from him. He is told: "Quick, forward, valiant soldier! Win for yourself a good name!" He does not know what he is about. His body is weak, his legs fail him. When victory is won, the captives are handed over to his majesty, to be taken to Egypt. The foreign woman faints on the march; she hangs herself on the soldier's neck. His knapsack drops, another grabs it while he is burdened with the woman. . . .

Be a scribe, and be spared from soldiering! You call and one says: "Here I am." You are safe from torments. Every man seeks to raise himself up. Take note of it!

WORKING WITH SOURCES

1. How does Nebmare-nakht attempt to make the life of a diligent scribe attractive to his apprentice? How does he use negative examples to steer Wenemdiamun in the right direction?
2. Why is the position of scribe so prominent in Middle Kingdom Egypt? What role does a scribe play in relation to the Pharaoh?

2.4 Sketch of the Palace Complex at Knossos, Minoan Crete, ca. 1700–1400 BCE

In 1900, Sir Arthur Evans discovered the remains of a vast palace complex on the island of Crete in the southern Aegean Sea. Christening the civilization "Minoan" after the legendary King Minos of Crete, Evans continued to excavate at Knossos and at other sites around the island. The palace at Knossos seems to have contained hundreds of rooms, including a throne room and storage spaces for food and cisterns for the collection of water. The legacy of Evans's work can be viewed at the visual archive held at the Ashmolean Museum in Oxford, England (http://sirarthurevans.ashmus.ox.ac.uk/), and there is a virtual tour of the site, provided by the British School at Athens (http://www.bsa.ac.uk/knossos/vrtour/).

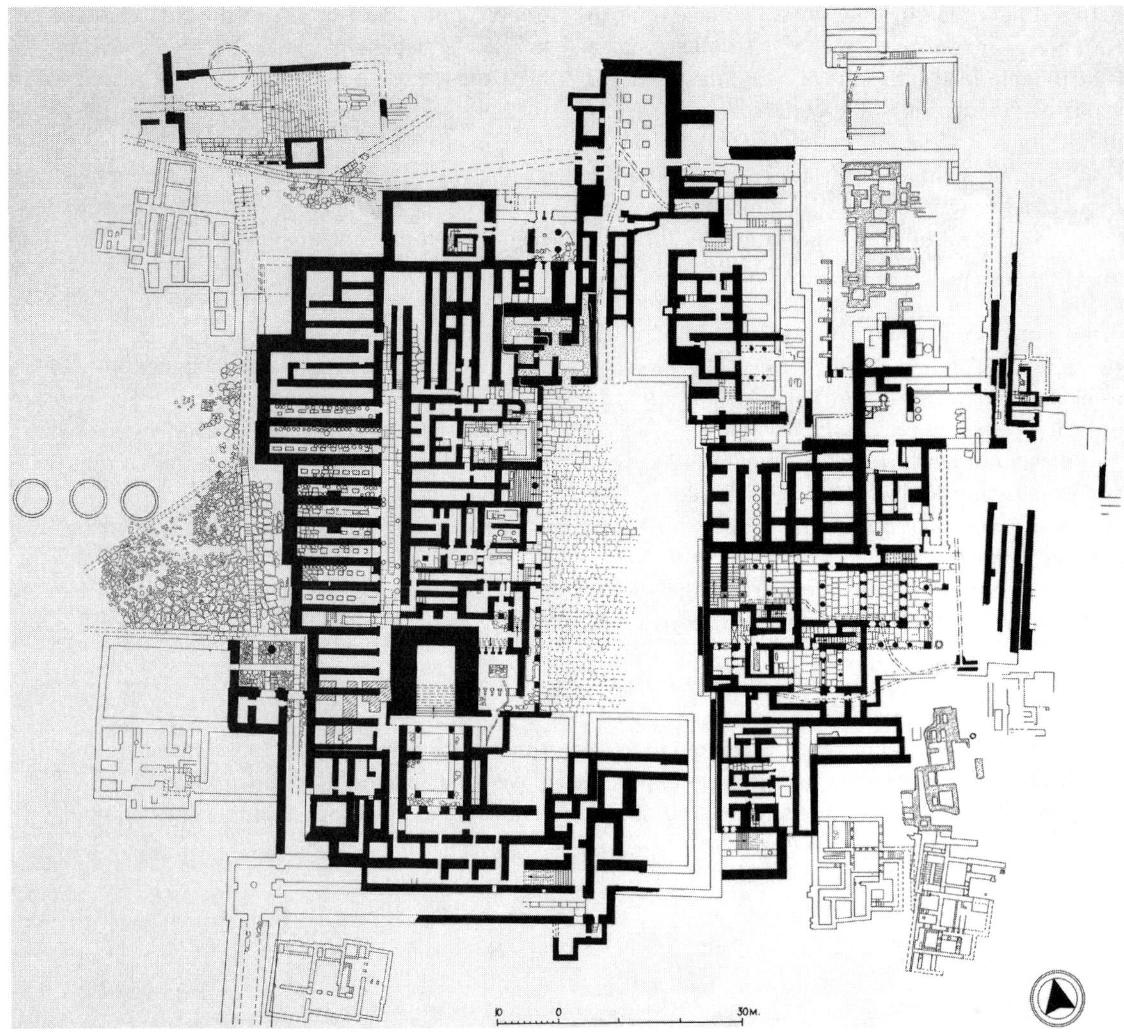

WORKING WITH SOURCES

1. Can the palace complex at Knossos be compared with palace sites in Mesopotamia and Egypt in the second millennium BCE? In what respects?
2. What do you think the palace complex suggests about the structure of Minoan society?

Source: © Ashmolean Museum, University of Oxford. AN.I.31 Plan of the Palace of Minos.

2.5 The Great Hymn to the Aten, ca. 1353–1336 BCE

This hymn to the Egyptian sun god Aten has been attributed to King Akhenaten ("the devoted adherent of Aten"), the Pharaoh formerly known as Amenhotep IV. While Akhenaten's experiment in monotheism was short-lived, the poem reflects the connections this revolutionary religious thinker attempted to forge between himself and an all-powerful deity. Note that he also solicits the blessings of Aten for himself, as leader of the Egyptian people, and for his wife, the famous Nefertiti.

Splendid you rise in heaven's lightland,
O living Aten, creator of life!
When you have dawned in eastern lightland,
You fill every land with your beauty.
You are beauteous, great, radiant,
High over every land;
Your rays embrace the lands,
To the limit of all that you made.

. . .

When you set in western lightland,
Earth is in darkness as if in death;
One sleeps in chambers, heads covered,
One eye does not see another.
Were they robbed of their goods,
That are under their heads,
People would not remark it.
Every lion comes from its den,
All the serpents bite;
Darkness hovers, earth is silent,
As their maker rests in lightland.

. . .

Ships fare north, fare south as well,
Roads lie open when you rise;
The fish in the river dart before you,
Your rays are in the midst of the sea.
Who makes seed grow in women,
Who creates people from sperm;
Who feeds the son in his mother's womb,
Who soothes him to still his tears.
Nurse in the womb,
Giver of breath,
To nourish all that he has made.

. . .

You are in my heart,
There is no other who knows you,
Only your son, ***Neferkheprure, Only-one-of-Re,***
Whom you have taught your ways and your
might.
[Those on] earth come from your hand as you
made them,
When you have dawned they live,
When you set they die;
You yourself are lifetime, one lives by you.
All eyes are on your beauty until you set.
All labor ceases when you rest in the west;
When you rise you stir [everyone] for
the King,
Every leg is on the move since you founded
the earth.
You rouse them for your son who came from
your body,
The King who lives by Maat, the Lord of the
Two Lands,
Neferkheprure, Only-one-of-Re,

Neferkheprure, Only-one-of-Re: Akhenaten.

Source: Translated by J. A. Wilson, as quoted by Miriam Lichtheim, *Ancient Egyptian Literature*, vol. 2, 96–99.

The Son of Re who lives by **Maat**, the Lord of crowns,
Akhenaten, great in his lifetime;
And the great Queen whom he loves, the Lady of the Two Lands,
Nefer-nefru-Aten Nefertiti, living forever.

WORKING WITH SOURCES

1. How does the hymn reflect on the practical advantages provided by the sun?
2. How does the hymn reinforce the power of Aten in political terms?

Maat: balance, law, justice.

3. SHIFTING AGRARIAN CENTERS IN INDIA, 3000–600 BCE

3.1 Hymns to Agni, from the *Rig-Veda*, Book 2, ca. 1400–900 BCE

The worship of Agni, as the fire principle animating a burnt offering to the gods, features prominently in the *Rig-Veda*. The voice of Agni was thought be heard in the crackling of the fire beneath a sacrifice, and it was a crucial element of Vedic tradition that the priest perform the ritual correctly. Fire was conflated with the emanations of the sun, and the priestly *varna*, or caste, was thought to be the community's best representative to the god.

HYMN I. AGNI

1 THOU, Agni, shining in thy glory through the days, art brought to life from out of the waters, from the stone:

From out of the forest trees and herbs that grow on ground, thou, Sovereign Lord of men art generated pure.

2 Thine is the Herald's task and Cleanser's duly timed; Leader art thou, and Kindler for the pious man.

Thou art Director, thou the ministering Priest: thou art the Brahman, Lord and Master in our home.

3 Hero of Heroes, Agni! Thou art Indra, thou art Viṣṇu of the Mighty Stride, adorable:

Thou, Brahmaṇaspati, the Brahman finding wealth: thou, O Sustainer, with thy wisdom tendest us.

4 Agni, thou art King Varuṇa whose laws stand fast; as Mitra, Wonder-Worker, thou must be implored.

Aryaman, heroes' Lord, art thou, enriching all, and liberal Aṃśa in the synod, O thou God.

. . .

12 Thou, Agni, cherished well, art highest vital power; in thy delightful hue are glories visible.

Thou art the lofty might that furthers each design: thou art wealth manifold, diffused on every side.

13 Thee, Agni, have the Ādityas taken as their mouth; the Pure Ones have made thee, O Sage, to be their tongue.

They who love offerings cling to thee at solemn rites: by thee the Gods devour the duly offered food.

14 By thee, O Agni, all the Immortal guileless Gods eat with thy mouth the oblation that is offered them.

By thee do mortal men give sweetness to their drink. Pure art thou born, the embryo of the plants of earth.

. . .

HYMN II. AGNI

1 WITH sacrifice exalt Agni who knows all life; worship him with oblation and the song of praise,

Well kindled, nobly fed; heaven's Lord, Celestial Priest, who labors at the pole where deeds of might are done.

2 At night and morning, Agni, have they called to thee, like milk-cattle in their stalls lowing to meet their young.

Source: The Hymns of the Rigveda, trans. Ralph T. H. Griffith (Benares: E. J. Lazarus, 1889), 333–338.

As messenger of heaven thou lightest all night long the families of men. Thou Lord of precious boons.

3 Him have the Gods established at the region's base, doer of wondrous deeds, Herald of heaven and earth;

Like a most famous car, Agni the purely bright, like Mitra to be glorified among the people.

4 Him have they set in his own dwelling, in the vault, like the Moon waxing, fulgent, in the realm of air.

Bird of the firmament, observant with his eyes, guard of the place as it were, looking to gods and men.

5 May he as Priest encompass all the sacrifice. Men throng to him with offerings and with hymns of praise.

Raging with jaws of gold among the growing plants, like heaven with all the stars, he quickens earth and sky.

. . .

12 Knower of all that lives, O Agni, may we both, singers of praise and chiefs, be in thy keeping still.

Help us to wealth exceeding good and glorious, abundant, rich in children and their progeny.

13 The princely worshippers who send to those who sing thy praise, O Agni, reward, graced with cattle and horses,—

Lead thou both these and us forward to higher bliss. With brave men in the assembly may we speak aloud.

WORKING WITH SOURCES

1. Why was the priestly caste so vital to the correct performance of the ritual?
2. How are the powers of the sun and a sacrificial fire conflated in these hymns?

3.2 The Bhagavad Gita, ca. 1750–800 BCE, Written Down in the Third Century BCE

The Bhagavad Gita comprises the sixth book, and is the central component, of the Mahabharata. Because it centers on the struggles between kings and princes, the Mahabharata can be read as a reflection of the ideological components of rulership in ancient India. At its center is a power struggle between the descendants of two brothers, culminating in a comprehensive war that ends in the victory of one branch of the family over the other. Elements of philosophy, religion, and moral behavior appear throughout the poem, and the concepts of *dharma* (natural law, correct behavior) and chaos are introduced by Krishna, the wise sage who appears at critical moments to explain the wider implications of what seems a simple battle narrative. The speakers in the following excerpt are Dhritarâshtra, a blind king in the midst of a succession crisis; Sañgaya, the visionary narrator of the battle; and Arjuna, one of the five sons of Pandu, the Pandava.

Source: The Bhagavadgita, with the Sanatsugatiya and the Anugita, trans. Kashinath Trimbak Telang (Oxford: Clarendon, 1882), 37, 39–41, 42, 73–75, 87–88, and 91.

BHAGAVADGÎTÂ. CHAPTER I

Dhritarâshtra said: What did my (people) and the Pândavas do, O Sañgaya! when they assembled together on the holy field of Kurukshetra, desirous to do battle?

. . .

Sañgaya said: Thus addressed by Gudâkesa , O descendant of Bharata! Hrishîkesa stationed that excellent chariot between the two armies, in front of Bhîshma and Drona and of all the kings of the earth, and said O son of Prithâ! Look at these assembled Kauravas.' There the son of Prithâ saw in both armies, fathers, and grandfathers, preceptors, maternal uncles, brothers, sons, grandsons, companions, fathers-in-law, as well as friends. And seeing all those kinsmen standing (there), the son of Kuntî [Arjuna] was overcome by excessive pity and spake thus despondingly.

Arjuna said: Seeing these kinsmen, O Krishna! standing (here) desirous to engage in battle, my limbs droop down; my mouth is quite dried up; a tremor comes on my body; and my hairs stand on end; the Gândîva (bow) slips from my hand; my skin burns intensely. I am unable, too, to stand up; my mind whirls round, as it were; O Kesava! I see adverse omens and I do not perceive any good (to accrue) after killing (my) kinsmen in the battle. I do not wish for victory, O Krishna! nor sovereignty, nor pleasures: what is sovereignty to us, O Govinda! what enjoyments, and even life? Even those, for whose sake we desire sovereignty, enjoyments, and pleasures, are standing here for battle, abandoning life and wealth-preceptors, fathers, sons as well as grandfathers, maternal uncles, fathers-in-law, grandsons, brothers-in-law, as also (other) relatives. These I do not wish to kill, though they kill (me), O destroyer of Madhu! Even for the sake of sovereignty over the three worlds, how much less than for this earth (alone)?

. . .

Sañgaya said: Having spoken thus, Arjuna cast aside his bow together with the arrows, on the battlefield, and sat down in (his) chariot, with a mind agitated by grief.

CHAPTER VII

The Deity said: O son of Prithâ! now hear how you can without doubt know me fully, fixing your mind on me, and resting in me, and practicing devotion. I will now tell you exhaustively about knowledge together with experience; that being known, there is nothing further left in this world to know. Among thousands of men, only some work for perfection; and even of those who have reached perfection, and who are assiduous, only some know me truly. . . .

There is nothing else, O Dhanañgaya! higher than myself; all this is woven upon me, like numbers of pearls upon a thread. I am the taste in water, O son of Kuntî! I am the light of the sun and moon. I am 'Om' in all the Vedas, sound in space, and manliness in human beings; I am the fragrant smell in the earth, refulgence in the fire; I am life in all beings, and penance in those who perform penance. Know me, O son of Prithâ! to be the eternal seed of all beings; I am the discernment of the discerning ones, and I the glory of the glorious. I am also the strength, unaccompanied by fondness or desire, of the strong. And, O chief of the descendants of Bharata! I am love unopposed to piety among all beings. And all entities which are of the quality of goodness, and those which are of the quality of passion and of darkness, know that they are, indeed, all from me; I am not in them, but they are in me. The whole universe deluded by these three states of mind, developed from the qualities, does not know me, who am beyond them and inexhaustible; for this delusion of mine, developed from the qualities, is divine and difficult to transcend. Those cross beyond this delusion who resort to me alone. Wicked men, doers of evil (acts), who are deluded, who are deprived of their knowledge by (this) delusion, and who incline to the demoniac state of mind, do not resort to me. But, O Arjuna! doers of good (acts) of four classes worship me: one who is distressed, one who is seeking after knowledge, one who wants wealth, and one, O chief of the descendants of Bharata! who is possessed of knowledge. Of these, he who is possessed of knowledge, who is always devoted, and whose worship is (addressed) to one (Being) only, is esteemed highest.

. . .

CHAPTER X

. . .

Arjuna said: You are the supreme Brahman, the supreme goal, the holiest of the holy. All sages, as well as the divine sage Nârada, Asita, Devala, and Vyâsa, call you the eternal being, divine, the first god, the unborn, the all-pervading. And so, too, you tell me yourself, O Kesava! I believe all this that you tell me (to be) true; for, O lord! neither the gods nor demons understand your manifestation. You only know yourself by yourself. O best of beings! creator of all things! lord of all things! god of gods! lord of the universe! be pleased to declare without exception your divine emanations, by which emanations you stand pervading all these worlds. How shall I know you, O you of mystic power! always meditating on you? And in what various entities, O lord! should I meditate on you? Again, O Ganârdana! do you yourself declare your powers and emanations; because hearing this nectar, I (still) feel no satiety.

The Deity said: . . . I am the rod of those that restrain, and the policy of those that desire victory. I am silence respecting secrets. I am the knowledge of those that have knowledge And, O Arjuna! I am also that which is the seed of all things. There is nothing movable or immovable which can exist without me. O terror of your foes! there is no end to my divine emanations. Here I have declared the extent of (those) emanations only in part. Whatever thing (there is) of power, or glorious, or splendid, know all that to be produced from portions of my energy.

WORKING WITH SOURCES

1. Why does Arjuna feel compelled to act, despite the competing claims of family ties?
2. How does the text develop the theme of supreme knowledge and its power?

3.3 The Brihadaranyaka Upanishad, ca. 600 BCE

A diverse set of writings, the Upanishads were thought to convey secret knowledge and serve as the *vedanta*, or fulfillment, of the Vedic tradition. Among these documents are the Aranyakas ("forest books"), which may have been recited originally by hermits who had retreated to forests. Throughout the Upanishads one can see the full development of the principle of the joining of the individual self (*atman*, or "soul") with the *brahman*, or "world soul"/ "soul essence."

SECOND ADHYÂYA. FIRST BRÂHMANA

1 There was formerly the proud Gârgya Bâlâki, a man of great reading. He said to Agâtasatru of Kâsi, 'Shall I tell you Brahman?' Agâtasatru said: 'We give a thousand (cows) for that speech (of yours), for verily all people run away, saying, Ganaka (the king of Mithilâ) is our father (patron).'

2 Gârgya said: 'The person that is in the sun, that I adore as Brahman.' Agâtasatru said to him: 'No, no! Do not speak to me on this. I adore him verily as the supreme, the head of all beings, the king. Whoso adores him thus, becomes Supreme, the head of all beings, a king.'

Source: The Upanishads, vol. 2, trans. F. Max Müller (Oxford: Clarendon, 1884), 100–101 and 103–105.

3 Gârgya said: 'The person that is in the moon (and in the mind), that I adore as Brahman.' Agâtasatru said to him: 'No, no! Do not speak to me on this. I adore him verily as the great, clad in white raiment, as Soma, the king.' Whoso adores him thus, Soma is poured out and poured forth for him day by day, and his food does not fail.

4 Gârgya said: 'The person that is in the lightning (and in the heart), that I adore as Brahman.' Agâtasatru said to him: 'No, no! Do not speak to me on this. I adore him verily as the luminous.' Whoso adores him thus, becomes luminous, and his offspring becomes luminous.

. . .

13 Gârgya said: 'The person that is in the body, that I adore as Brahman.' Agâtasatru said to him: 'No, no! Do not speak to me on this. I adore him verily as embodied.' Whoso adores him thus, becomes embodied, and his offspring becomes embodied. Then Gârgya became silent.

14 Agâtasatru said: 'Thus far only?' 'Thus far only,' he replied. Agâtasatru said: 'This does not suffice to know it (the true Brahman).' Gârgya replied: 'Then let me come to you, as a pupil.'

15 Agâtasatru said: 'Verily, it is unnatural that a Brâhmana should come to a **Kshatriya**, hoping that he should tell him the Brahman. However, I shall make you know him clearly,' thus saying he took him by the hand and rose.

And the two together came to a person who was asleep. He called him by these names, 'Thou, great one, clad in white raiment, Soma, King.' He did not rise. Then rubbing him with his hand, he woke him, and he arose.

16 Agâtasatru said: 'When this man was thus asleep, where was then the person (purusha), the intelligent? And from whence did he thus come back?' Gârgya did not know this?

17 Agâtasatru said: 'When this man was thus asleep, then the intelligent person (purusha), having through the intelligence of the senses (prânas) absorbed within himself all intelligence, lies in the ether, which is in the heart. When he takes in these different kinds of intelligence, then it is said that the man sleeps (svapiti). Then the breath is kept in, speech is kept in, the ear is kept in, the eye is kept in, the mind is kept in.

18 But when he moves about in sleep (and dream), then these are his worlds. He is, as it were, a great king; he is, as it were, a great Brâhmana; he rises, as it were, and he falls. And as a great king might keep in his own subjects, and move about, according to his pleasure, within his own domain, thus does that person (who is endowed with intelligence) keep in the various senses (prânas) and move about, according to his pleasure, within his own body (while dreaming).

19 Next, when he is in profound sleep, and knows nothing, there are the seventy-two thousand arteries called Hita, which from the heart spread through the body. Through them he moves forth and rests in the surrounding body. And as a young man, or a great king, or a great Brâhmana, having reached the summit of happiness, might rest, so does he then rest.

20 As the spider comes out with its thread, or as small sparks come forth from fire, thus do all senses, all worlds, all Devas, all beings come forth from that Self The Upanishad (the true name and doctrine) of that Self is 'the True of the True.' Verily the senses are the true, and he is the true of the true.

Kshatriya: Second highest of the four *varnas* (castes) in Hindu society.

WORKING WITH SOURCES

1. How does the text develop the principles of *brahman* and *soma* addressed in Chapter 3?
2. What is the responsibility of the king with respect to knowledge?

3.4 The *Code of Manu*, ca. 100–300 CE

The *Code of Manu* deals with many different features of Hindu life, such as the proper behavior of different castes and methods for ritual purification. The "Manu" referred to in the title is the legendary "first man" of Hindu culture, also recognized as the first lawgiver. Thus, the *Code of Manu* is thought of within Hinduism as a text based on human traditions (*smriti*), but it is also believed to be consistent with the values included in texts that are divinely revealed (*shruti*), such as the "Purusha Hymn." As a result, it restates and reaffirms traditional values and structures, but it does so on the basis of religious authority.

The responsibilities described for women in the *Code of Manu* need to be understood within the context of Hinduism. As was discussed in Chapter 3, a central component of Hinduism is the concept of *dharma* ("that which is firm"). Hindus believe that by living up to the religious and social responsibilities attached to one's social position (caste and gender), one sustains the proper order of the universe and gains good *karma*, moving up the scale of reincarnation toward unity with the *brahman*, or World Soul. Composed following a period of unrest, the *Code of Manu* represents a vigorous attempt to reestablish order within the Hindu world.

Hear now the duties of women.

By a girl, by a young woman, or even by an aged one, nothing must be done independently, even in her own house.

Her lord is dead to her sons; a woman must never be independent.

She must not seek to separate herself from her father, husband, or sons; by leaving them she would make both (her own and her husband's) families contemptible.

She must always be cheerful, clever in (the management of her) household affairs, careful in cleaning her utensils, and economical in expenditure.

Him to whom her father may give her, or her brother with the father's permission, she shall obey as long as he lives, and when he is dead, she must not insult (his memory). . . .

[B]etrothal (by the father or guardian) is the cause of (the husband's) dominion (over his wife).

The husband who wedded her with sacred texts, always gives happiness to his wife, both in season and out of season, in this world and in the next.

Though destitute of virtue, or seeking pleasure (elsewhere), or devoid of good qualities, (yet) a husband must be constantly worshipped as a god by a faithful wife.

No sacrifice, no vow, no fast must be performed by women apart (from their husbands); if a wife obeys her husband, she will for that (reason alone) be exalted in heaven.

A faithful wife, who desires to dwell (after death) with her husband, must never do anything that might displease him who took her hand, whether he be alive or dead. . . . [L]et her emaciate her body by (living on) pure flowers, roots, and fruit; but she must never even mention the name of another man after her husband has died.

Until death let her be patient (of hardships), self-controlled, and chaste, and strive (to fulfill) that most excellent duty which (is prescribed) for wives who have one husband only. A virtuous wife who after the death of her husband constantly remains chaste, reaches heaven, though she have no son, just like those chaste men.

Source: The Law of Manu, in *The Sacred Books of the East*, vol. 25, trans. G. Bühler (Oxford: Clarendon, 1886), 194–197, 328–330, 332, 335, 344–345.

By violating her duty towards her husband, a wife is disgraced in this world, (after death) she enters the womb of a jackal, and is tormented by diseases (the punishment of) her sin. . . .

[A] female who controls her thoughts, speech, and actions, gains in this (life) highest renown, and in the next (world) a place near her husband.

Women must particularly be guarded against evil inclinations, however trifling (they may appear); for, if they are not guarded, they will bring sorrow on two families. . . . No man can completely guard women by force; but they can be guarded by the . . . (following) expedients: Let the (husband) employ his (wife) in the collection and expenditure of his wealth, in keeping (everything) clean, in (the fulfillment of) religious duties, in the preparation of his food, and in looking after the household utensils. Women, confined in the house under trustworthy and obedient servants, are not (well) guarded; but those who of their own accord keep guard over themselves, are well guarded. . . .

Through their passion for men, through their mutable temper, through their natural heartlessness, they become disloyal towards their husbands, however carefully they may be guarded in this (world).

(When creating them) Manu allotted to women (a love of their) bed, (of their) seat and (of) ornament, impure desires, wrath, dishonesty, malice, and bad conduct. . . . The production of children, the nurture of those born, and the daily life of men, (of these matters) woman is visibly the cause.

Offspring, (the due performance of) religious rites, faithful service, highest conjugal happiness and heavenly bliss for the ancestors and oneself, depend on one's wife alone.

He only is a perfect man who consists (of three persons united), his wife, himself, and his offspring; thus (says the Veda), and (learned) Brahmanas propound this (maxim) likewise, "The husband is declared to be one with the wife." . . .

The husband receives his wife from the gods, (he does not wed her) according to his own will; doing what is agreeable to the gods, he must always support her (while she is) faithful.

"Let mutual fidelity continue until death," this may be considered as the summary of the highest law for husband and wife.

WORKING WITH SOURCES

1. According to the code, how should men relate to women? In what ways are men asked, in their relationships with women, to keep order?
2. How are women rewarded for behaving the way the code instructs them to? How are the rewards connected with the Hindu belief in reincarnation and *karma*?

3.5 Image of Draupadi and the Pandava, from the Dashavatara Temple, Deogarh, India, Late Sixth Century CE

This is an inscribed rendering of some of the major male and female characters of the Mahabharata. According to this legend, a king surrenders power to his blind brother and has five sons (the Pandava) by his queen, Kunti. The five brothers are collectively married to the beautiful princess Draupadi. In Indian tradition, her role is analogous to the way the palm of a hand holds together the hand's five fingers.

Source: Courtesy of Ed Sentne.

WORKING WITH SOURCES

1. How is the female principle represented in this collective portrait?
2. Does this image evoke in any way the restrictions on female behavior detailed in the *Code of Manu*?

4. AGRARIAN CENTERS AND THE MANDATE OF HEAVEN IN ANCIENT CHINA, 5000–481 BCE

4.1 *The Zuo Commentary* (*Zuozhuan*), ca. Fourth Century BCE

The *Spring and Autumn Annals* (*Chunqiu*), a chronicle covering the years 722–483 BCE and composed at the court of Lu (the home state of Confucius), was acknowledged even at the time to be very difficult reading. Accordingly, scholars began composing commentaries to elucidate its finer points and clarify its meaning. The third orthodox commentary, attributed to "Mr. Zuo," continues to influence historical thought about ancient China. This section concerns a conflict between the states of Qin and Jin in the seventh century BCE.

On ***renxu*** day, they fought on the plain of Han. The warhorses of Jin were confounded by the mud and forced to halt. The Lord [of Jin] called for Qing Zheng. Qing Zheng said, "You rejected my remonstrance and disobeyed the divination. You were resolutely seeking defeat—why flee from it now?" Then he abandoned [his lord].

Liang Youmi was driving for Han Jian; Guo She was the right-hand man. They came upon the carriage of the Earl of Qin and were about to stop him. [Qing] Zheng misled them by [calling for someone] to save the Lord [of Jin]; thus they lost the Earl of Qin. Qin caught the Marquis of Jin and returned with him. The Grand Masters of Jin followed him, letting their hair loose and camping in the wilderness. The Earl of Qin sent an embassy [asking them] to desist, saying, "Gentlemen, why are you so aggrieved? I am accompanying the Lord of Jin to the west only in order to comply with the ominous dream of Jin. Would I dare do anything excessive?"

The Grand Masters of Jin paid their respects by kowtowing three times and said, "Lord, you tread on the Earth Deity and bear up August Heaven. August Heaven and the Earth Deity have surely heard your words, my Lord, so we, your flock of subjects, dare to be inspired by them beneath you."

When Lady Mu heard that the Marquis of Jin was about to arrive, she ascended a terrace with Heir Apparent Ying, [her other son] Hong, and her daughter Jianbi, and stood upon a pyre there. She sent an embassy clad in mourning cap and gown to meet [her husband], and then she said, "Heaven Above has sent down catastrophe, causing my two lords to meet each other without jade and silk, and to be aroused to warfare. If the Lord of Jin enters [the capital] in the morning, I and my children will die in the evening; if he enters in the evening, we will die the next morning. Only my Lord can decide [the hour of my death]!" Thereupon [the Lord of Jin] was lodged in the Spirit Terrace.

. . .

Zisang said, "If we send him home but take his heir apparent hostage, that would be the greatest

Renxu: The date of the battle.

Source: Victor H. Mair, Nancy Shatzman Steinhardt, and Paul R. Goldin, eds., *Hawai'i Reader in Traditional Chinese Culture* (Honolulu: University of Hawai'i Press, 2005), 72–76.

accomplishment. Jin cannot be annihilated, and to kill their lord would only bring about their hatred. Moreover, Historian Yi once said, 'Do not initiate misfortune; do not await [others'] disorders; do not redouble anger.' Redoubled anger is difficult to bear, and to abuse others is inauspicious." Thereupon they granted peace with Jin.

WORKING WITH SOURCES

1. Is this merely a rousing battle story, or does the tale convey a sense of what behavior is proper in the midst of conflict?
2. What role does anger play in the narrative? Why?

4.2 Excerpts from *The Book of Odes* (*Shi Jing*), ca. 2852–481 BCE

Over 300 poems of various lengths were anthologized and transmitted by Confucius in the early fifth century BCE. Philosophers of the Confucian school (see Chapter 9) cherished the *Odes* and cited them frequently, and they have continued to entrance readers with their naturalistic imagery and personal voices. Only two samples are given here, but this rich tradition of poetry should be sampled at length.

WILD AND WINDY

Wild and windy was the day;
You looked at me and laughed,
But the jest was cruel, and the laughter mocking.
My heart within is sore.

There was a great sandstorm that day;
Kindly you made as though to come,
Yet neither came nor went away.
Long, long my thoughts.

A great wind and darkness;
Day after day it is dark.
I lie awake, cannot sleep,
And gasp with longing.

Dreary, dreary the gloom;
The thunder growls.
I lie awake, cannot sleep,
And am destroyed with longing.

I BEG YOU, ZHONG ZI

I beg of you, Zhong Zi,
Do not climb into our homestead,
Do not break the willows we have planted.
Not that I mind about the willows,
But I am afraid of my father and mother.
Zhong Zi I dearly love;
But of what my father and mother say
Indeed I am afraid.

I beg of you, Zhong Zi,
Do not climb over the wall,
Do not break the mulberry-trees we have planted.
Not that I mind about the mulberry-trees,

Source: The Book of Songs, transl. Arthur Waley, edited with additional translations by Joseph R. Allen (New York: Grove, 1996), 27 and 65.

But I am afraid of my brothers.
Zhong Zi I dearly love;
But of what my brothers say
Indeed I am afraid.

I beg of you, Zhong Zi,
Do not climb into our garden,
Do not break the hard-wood we have planted.
Not that I mind about the hard-wood,

But I am afraid of what people will say.
Zhong Zi I dearly love;
But of all that people will say
Indeed I am afraid.

WORKING WITH SOURCES

1. How do the poems deal with the theme of love, whether reciprocated or not?
2. What do they suggest about gender relations in ancient China?

4.3 *The Book of Lord Shang (Shang Chün Shu)*, ca. 338 BCE

This collection of sayings and reports attributed to Lord Shang (d. 338 BCE) may have been compiled by later officials, but its vision of a centralized bureaucracy was emulated at many points in China's turbulent history. The work is composed of 25 or more brief sections, some of which are lost, but the remainder address the necessity of good and competent government.

The guiding principles of the people are base and they are not consistent in what they value. As the conditions in the world change, different principles are practiced. Therefore it is said that there is a fixed standard in a king's principles. Indeed, a king's principles represent one viewpoint and those of a minister another. The principles each follows are different but are one in both representing a fixed standard. Therefore, it is said: "When the people are stupid, by knowledge one may rise to supremacy; when the world is wise, by force one may rise to supremacy." That means that when people are stupid, there are plenty of strong men but not enough wise, and when the world is wise, there are plenty of clever men, but not enough strong. It is the nature of people, when they have no knowledge, to study, and when they have no strength, to submit.

. . .

A sage-prince understands what is essential in affairs, and therefore in his administration of the people, there is that which is most essential. For the fact that uniformity in the manipulating of rewards and punishments supports moral virtue is connected with human psychology. A sage-prince, by his ruling of men, is certain to win their hearts; consequently he is able to use force. Force produces strength, strength produces prestige, prestige produces virtue, and so virtue has its origin in force, which a sage-prince alone possesses, and therefore he is able

Source: Sebastian De Grazia, ed., *Masters of Chinese Political Thought: From the Beginnings to the Han Dynasty* (New York: Viking, 1973), 339–343.

to transmit benevolence and righteousness to the empire.

. . .

Of old, the one who could regulate the empire was he who regarded as his first task the regulating of his own people; the one who could conquer a strong enemy was he who regarded as his first task the conquering of his own people. For the way in which the conquering of the people is based upon the regulating of the people, is like the effect of smelting in regard to metal or the work of the potter in regard to clay; if the basis is not solid, then people are like flying birds or like animals. Who can regulate these? The basis of the people is the law. Therefore, a good ruler obstructed the people by means of the law, and so his reputation and his territory flourished.

WORKING WITH SOURCES

1. Why does Lord Shang assume there will be an antagonistic relationship between a ruler and the ruled?
2. Would he think it preferable for a leader to appear virtuous rather than to actually be virtuous?

4.4 *The Canon of Shun,* Third Millennium BCE?

Shun was thought to be one of the three "Sage Kings" who ruled China between 2852 and 2205 BCE, after the reign of the "Yellow Emperor." The achievements of these kings are recorded—though the exact dating of each strand of material is controversial—in the *Shujing*, or *Book of History*. The material in the compilation purportedly dates from 2357 to 631 BCE, but, regardless of its precise chronology, the "Canon" attributed to Shun reveals increased sophistication in determining the role and proper behavior of a leader.

1 Examining into antiquity, we find the emperor Shun was called Chong Hua. He corresponded to the former emperor; he was profound, wise, accomplished, and intelligent. He was mild and respectful, and entirely sincere. The report of his mysterious virtue was heard on high, and he was appointed to occupy the imperial Seat.

. . .

9 In five years there was one tour of inspection, and four appearances of the nobles at court. They set forth a report of their government in words. This was clearly tested by their works. They received chariots and robes according to their services.

10 Shun instituted the division of the land into twelve provinces, raising altars upon twelve hills in them. He likewise deepened the rivers.

11 He gave delineations of the statutory punishments, enacting banishment as a mitigation of the five great inflictions, with the whip to be employed in the magistrates' courts, the stick to be employed in schools, and money to be received for redeemable crimes. Inadvertent offenses and those which might be caused by misfortune were to be pardoned, but those who offended presumptuously or repeatedly were to be punished with death. "Let me be reverent;

Source: James Legge, trans., *The Sacred Books of China: The Texts of Confucianism*, vol. 3 (Oxford: Clarendon, 1879), 38, 40–41, and 44–45.

let me be reverent!" he said to himself. "Let compassion rule in punishment!"

. . .

24 The emperor said, "Kui, I appoint you to be Director of music, and to teach our sons, so that the straightforward may yet be mild, the gentle may yet be dignified, the strong not tyrannical, and the impetuous not arrogant. Poetry is the expression of earnest thought; singing is the prolonged utterance of that expression. The notes accompany that utterance, and they are harmonized themselves by the pitch pipes. In this way the eight different kinds of instruments can all be adjusted so that one shall not take from or interfere with another, and spirits and men will thereby be brought into harmony." Kui said, "Oh! I smite the stone; I smite the stone. The various animals lead on one another to dance."

25 The emperor said, "Long, I abominate slanderous speakers, and destroyers of right ways, who agitate and alarm my people. I appoint you to be the minister of Communication. Early and late give forth my orders and report to me, seeing that everything is true."

26 The emperor said, "Ah! you, twenty and two men, be reverent, and so shall you aid me in performing the service of heaven."

27 Every three years there was an examination of merits, and after three examinations the undeserving were degraded, and the deserving promoted. By this arrangement the duties of all the departments were fully discharged. The people of San Miao were discriminated and separated.

28 In the thirtieth year of his life, Shun was called to employment. Thirty years he was on the throne with Yao. Fifty years after he went on high and died.

WORKING WITH SOURCES

1. How important is effective management of subordinates to the career of a king of Shun's stature?
2. To which particular voices should a wise king give heed?

4.5 Iron Sword with Jade Handle, Earliest Cast-Iron Object (Western Zhou), from Henan Museum, Guo State, Sanmenxia City, ca. 1046–771 BCE

When this sword was discovered in 1990, it challenged conventional wisdom about when and under what circumstances Chinese people made the first cast-iron object. The dating of the object to the Western Zhou period pushed back the earliest date of this kind of manufacture by over 200 years. The sword consists of an iron blade, a bronze handle core, and a jade handle. Embedded turquoises were also found at the joint of the blade and the handle.

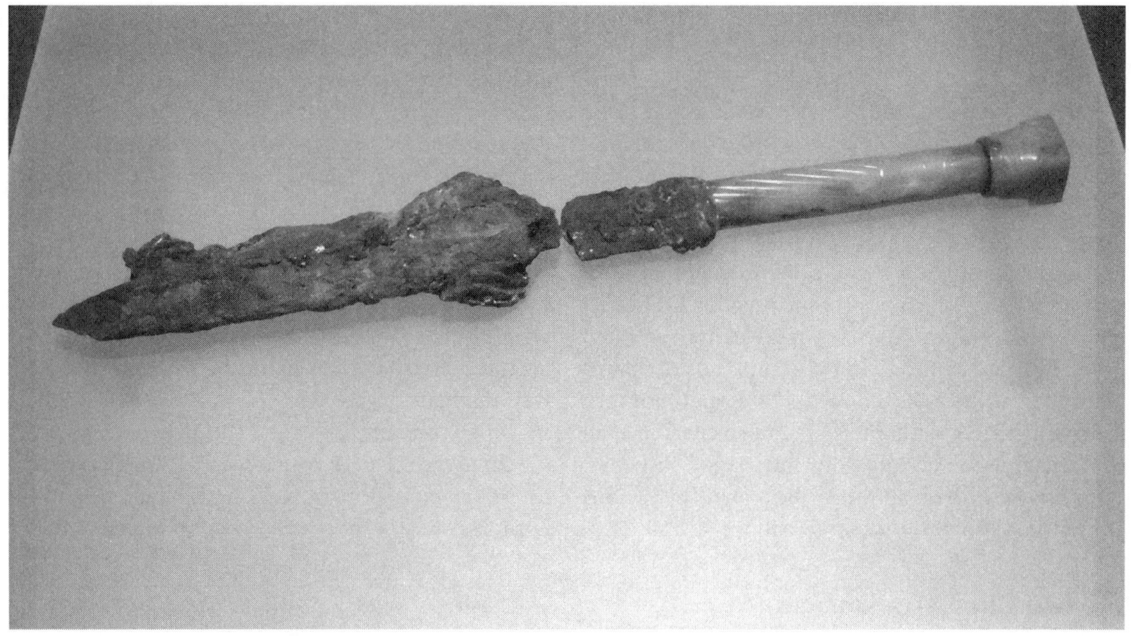

WORKING WITH SOURCES

1. What does this object suggest about the casting technology and metalworking prowess of workers in the Zhou dynasty?
2. Why would a cast-iron sword have been an especially effective weapon in this era?

Source: Tim Hulsen - OurTravelPics.com

5. ORIGINS APART: THE AMERICAS AND OCEANIA, 30,000–600 BCE

5.1 *Quipú* from the Caral-Supé Culture, Peru, 2600–2000 BCE

Recent archaeological discoveries in the Caral-Supé valley have pushed back the timeline of cultural development in the Andes by several millennia. A fixture of later Incan culture, the *quipú* was an elaborate series of knotted ropes that seemed to serve as a coded system of communication. Excavations have demonstrated that the *quipú* was used in the region as much as 3,000 years before its earliest previous attestation. Moreover, this *quipú* was apparently left as an offering on the stairway of a public building when another building was built on top.

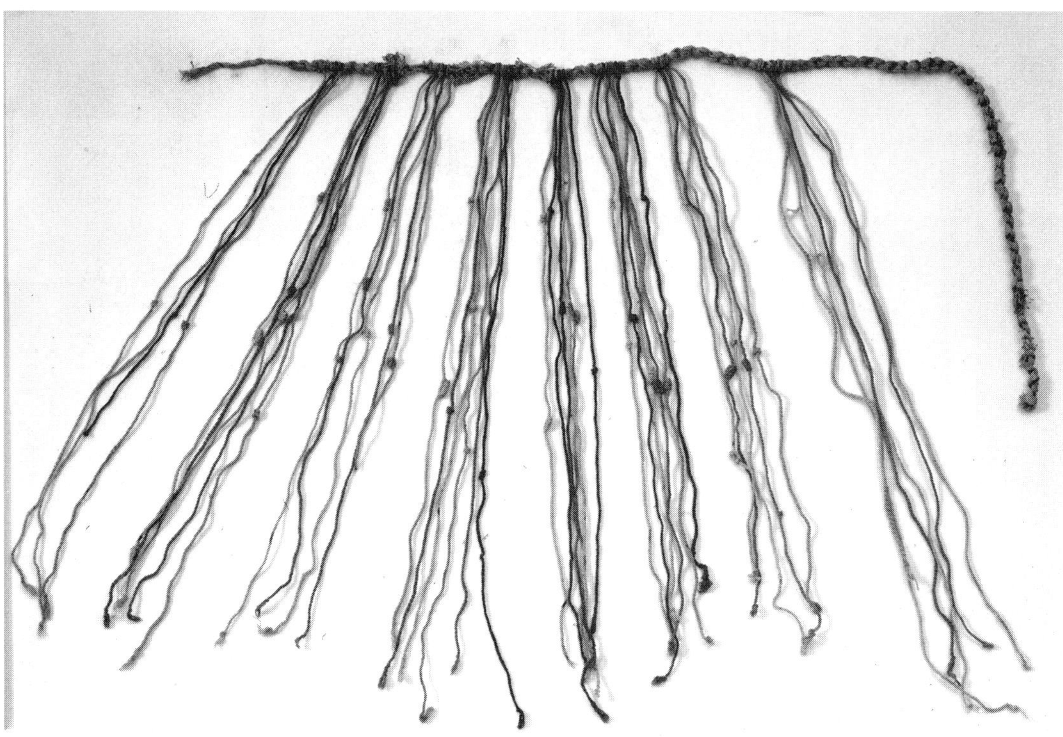

Source: © President and Fellows of Harvard College, Peabody Museum of Archaeology and Ethnology, Harvard University, PM# 2004.24.35177 (digital file# 153390016).

WORKING WITH SOURCES

1. What does this object suggest about the continuities among various Andean cultures over several thousand years?
2. What does the existence of an object used for accounting suggest about this culture's administrative and bureaucratic sophistication?

5.2 Textile Fragment from Chavín de Huántar, Peru, ca. 500–200 BCE

Now housed in the Metropolitan Museum of Art in New York City, this section of an elaborately crafted and painted piece of textile attests the manufacturing prowess of the Chavín people. In the image, a central fanged figure grasps and may be controlling a four-eyed monster. The snake-like elements of this figure have led to the conclusion that he is an ancestor of the *khipucamayuc*, the Inca name for the keeper of a *quipú*.

WORKING WITH SOURCES

1. What does the sophistication of this object indicate about the division of labor in Chavín society at its peak?
2. What were the likely connections between textile manufacture and the operation of *quipú* in the period?

Source: © The Metropolitan Museum of Art/Art Resource, NY.

5.3 Burial Mound at L'Anse Amour, Labrador, Canada, ca. 5500 BCE

This mound marks the grave of an adolescent boy from the "Maritime Archaic" people of Labrador. Roughly 7,500 years ago, his body was wrapped in a shroud of bark or hide and placed face down in the grave with his head facing to the west. At that point, a large mound of rocks was erected over his burial place.

WORKING WITH SOURCES

1. What are the similarities between this burial mound and others found in ancient North America?
2. What seems to have been the status of this boy, judging from the placement and the circumstances of his burial?

Source: Courtesy of Brian Bursey.

5.4 Lapita Pot Shards, found in Vanuatu, Western Pacific, ca. Fourth Millennium BCE

Named for a site in the archipelago of New Caledonia, the Lapita culture was a system of kinship-based exchanges among the inhabitants of thousands of islands in the western Pacific. Elements of "Lapita ware," decorated with stamped patterns, were in high demand, and pots were exchanged among the inhabitants of the islands.

WORKING WITH SOURCES

1. What do the elaborate designs imprinted on this pot suggest about the sophistication of Lapita culture?
2. How can the pot be connected with the themes of navigation and gift exchange in the wider Polynesian culture?

Source: © Philippe Metois.

6. CHIEFDOMS AND EARLY STATES IN AFRICA AND THE AMERICAS, 600 BCE–600 CE

6.1 Relief Sculpture from Meroë, Sudan, ca. 600–300 BCE

The kings of Meroë, successors of the Nubia-descended 25th dynasty of Egypt, established their capital on the Middle Nile about 100 miles north of Khartoum, Sudan. At its height, the city was home to more than 20,000 people. Its surviving buildings have qualified it as a UNESCO World Heritage Site.

Source: ©Unesco/Ron Van Oers.

WORKING WITH SOURCES

1. How does the relief reflect the ongoing influence of ancient Egyptian iconography and symbolism?
2. What was the extent of the empire around Meroë, and what was the source of its influence?

6.2 Cosmas Indicopleustes (Cosmas the India-Voyager), *Christian Topography*, ca. 550 CE

This remarkable account of a merchant's travels throughout Eastern Africa, the Arabian Peninsula, and India resulted from the singular obsession of a monk in retirement. Determined to prove that a proper understanding of Earth's geography would confirm God's creation—and that the earth was a flat, oblong table surrounded by the ocean—the monk Cosmas reflected back on his extensive voyages, which had probably been undertaken to further a spice-import business. Cosmas commented on the trading practices of the Aksumites and on their wealthy culture, providing one of the few available outsider glimpses of Aksum.

The region that produces frankincense is situated at the projecting parts of Ethiopia, and lies inland, but is washed by the ocean on the other side. Hence the inhabitants of Barbaria, being near at hand, go up into the interior and, engaging in traffic with the natives, bring back from them many kinds of spices, frankincense, cassia, calamus, and many other articles of merchandise, which they afterwards send by sea to Agau, to the country of the Homerites [Yemen], to Further India, and to Persia.

This very fact you will find mentioned in the Book of Kings, where it is recorded that the Queen of Sheba, that is, of the Homerite country, whom afterwards our Lord in the Gospels calls the Queen of the South, brought to Solomon spices from this very Barbaria, which lay near Sheba on the other side of the sea, together with bars of ebony, and apes and gold from Ethiopia which, though separated from Sheba by the Arabian Gulf, lay in its vicinity. We can see again from the words of the Lord that he calls these places the ends of the earth, saying: *The Queen of the South shall rise up in judgment with this generation and shall condemn it, for she came from the ends of the earth to hear the wisdom of Solomon* (Matthew 12:42). For the Homerites are not far distant from Barbaria, as the sea which lies between them can be crossed in a couple of days, and then beyond Barbaria is the ocean, which is there called Zingion. The country known as that of Sasu is itself near the ocean, just as the ocean is near the frankincense country, in which there are many gold mines.

The King of the Aksumites, accordingly, every other year, through the governor of Agau, sends thither special agents to bargain for the gold, and these are accompanied by many other traders—upwards, say, of five hundred—bound on the same errand as themselves. They take along with them to the mining district oxen, lumps of salt, and iron, and when they reach its neighborhood they make a halt at a certain spot and form an encampment, which they fence

Source: Cosmas Indicopleustes, *Christianike Topographia*, Book 3, trans. and ed. Christopher Haas, Villanova University; available online: http://www29.homepage.villanova.edu/christopher.haas/cosmas_indicopleustes.htm.

round with a great hedge of thorns. Within this they live, and having slaughtered the oxen, cut them in pieces, and lay the pieces on the top of the thorns, along with the lumps of salt and the iron. Then come the natives bringing gold in nuggets like peas, called *tancharas*, and lay one or two or more of these upon what pleases them—the pieces of flesh or the salt or the iron, and then they retire to some distance off. Then the owner of the meat approaches, and if he is satisfied he takes the gold away, and upon seeing this, its owner comes and takes the flesh or the salt or the iron. If, however, he is not satisfied, he leaves the gold. When the native, seeing that he has not taken it comes and either puts down more gold, or takes up what he had laid down, and goes away.

Such is the mode in which business is transacted with the people of that country, because their language is different and interpreters are hardly to be found. The time they stay in that country is five days more or less, according as the natives more or less readily coming forward buy up all their wares. On the journey homeward they all agree to travel well-armed, since some of the tribes through whose country they must pass might threaten to attack them from a desire to rob them of their gold. The space of six months is taken up with this trading expedition, including both the going and the returning. In going they march very slowly, chiefly because of the cattle, but in returning they quicken their pace lest on the way they should be overtaken by winter and its rains.

For the sources of the river Nile lie somewhere in these parts, and in winter, on account of the heavy rains, the numerous rivers which they generate obstruct the path of the traveler. The people there have their winter at the time we have our summer. It begins in the month *Epiphi* of the Egyptians and continues till *Thoth*, and during the three months the rain falls in torrents, and makes a multitude of rivers all of which flow into the Nile.

WORKING WITH SOURCES

1. How does Cosmas characterize the Aksumites, and to what other peoples does he compare them?
2. How and why does Cosmas allude to Old and New Testament accounts in his analysis of cultures adjoining the Red Sea?

6.3 The Market at Jenné-jeno, Mali Founded, ca. Third Century BCE

After extensive archaeological work was done at the site of Jenné-jeno in the 1980s, researchers concluded that the city was the oldest known in sub-Saharan Africa, and that it flourished throughout the first millennium CE. It is situated on a vast low mound at the heart of the Niger Delta. The site was gradually abandoned in favor of Timbuktu during the Middle Ages.

Source: Photo by Rob Dougall.

WORKING WITH SOURCES

1. How did the founders of Jenné-jeno capitalize on existing trade networks in western Africa, and what geographic factors were involved?
2. Examining this recent photo of Jenné-jeno, what does it say about the continuity of patterns of trade and urbanism in West Africa?

6.4 Limestone Panel from a Mayan Temple, Palenque, ca. 490 CE

This panel from a temple in the Mayan city of Palenque contains glyphs (forming a caption) and two figures. A captive kneels before a standing warrior who holds a flint spear and wears a war headdress. The large text to the left records an event at Palenque that occurred in 490. The small text above the kneeling figure gives the name of a captive.

Source: The Linda Schele Drawings Collection, http://research.famsi.org/schele_list.php?_allSearch=118.

WORKING WITH SOURCES

1. What are the likely circumstances surrounding the creation of this image?
2. What were the connections between Mayan temples and warfare?

7. PERSIA, GREECE, AND ROME, 550 BCE–600 CE

7.1 The Cyrus Cylinder, 539 BCE

Founder of the Achaemenid Persian Empire, Cyrus (Kurosh) the Great rose to the throne of a small kingdom in 559 BCE; by the time of his death in 529, he had brought virtually the entire Near East under his control. In 539, he conquered Babylon and drove out Nabonidus, the last of the Neo-Babylonian kings. However, he was hailed as a liberator by the priests of the Babylonian god Marduk, and he issued a remarkable document, guaranteeing freedom of religion to the subjects whom he had added to his empire. The text, which was publicized in Akkadian, an ancient Mesopotamian language, is preserved on a clay cylinder, today called the Cyrus Cylinder and housed in the British Museum.

. . .

On account of their complaints, the lords of the gods became furiously angry and left their [the Babylonians'] land; the gods, who dwelt among them, left their homes. . . . In all lands everywhere [the god Marduk] searched; he looked through them and sought a righteous prince after his own heart, whom he took by the hand. He called Cyrus, king of Anshan, by name; he appointed him to lordship over the whole world.

The land of Qutu, all the Umman-manda, he cast down at his feet. The black-headed people, whom he gave his hands to conquer, he took them in justice and righteousness. Marduk, the great lord, looked joyously on the caring for his people, on his pious works and his righteous heart. To his city, Babylon, he caused [Cyrus] to go; he made him take the road to Babylon, going as a friend and companion at his side. His numerous troops, in unknown numbers, like the waters of a river, marched armed at his side. Without battle and conflict, he permitted him to enter Babylon. He spared his city, Babylon, a calamity. Nabonidus, the king, who did not fear him, he delivered into his hand.

. . .

When I [Cyrus] made my triumphal entrance into Babylon, I took up my lordly residence in the royal palace with joy and rejoicing; Marduk, the great lord, moved the noble heart of the residents of Babylon to me, while I gave daily attention to his worship. My numerous troops marched peacefully into Babylon. In all Sumer and Akkad I permitted no enemy to enter.

The needs of Babylon and of all its cities I gladly attended to. The people of Babylon [and . . .], and the shameful yoke was removed from them. Their dwellings, which had fallen, I restored. I cleared out their ruins. Marduk, the great lord, rejoiced in my pious deeds, and graciously blessed me, Cyrus, the king who worships him, and Cambyses, my own son, and all my troops, while we, before him, joyously praised his exalted godhead.

. . .

And the gods of Sumer and Akkad—whom Nabonidus, to the anger of the lord of the gods, had brought into Babylon—by the command of Marduk, the great lord, I caused them to take up their dwelling in residences that gladdened the heart. May all the gods, whom I brought into their cities, pray daily before Bel and Nabu for long life for me, and may they speak a gracious word for me and say to Marduk, my lord, "May Cyrus, the king who worships you, and Cambyses his son, their [. . .] I permitted all to dwell in peace [. . .].

Source: Rogers, Robert William. Cuneiform Parallels to the Old Testament, 1912. Reprinted, Ancient Texts and Translations. (Wipf & Stock, 2005), pg. 380–84. Used by permission of Wipf and Stock Publishers. www.wipfandstock.com

WORKING WITH SOURCES

1. How and why did Cyrus incorporate local deities into his public image after subjugating Babylon?
2. How does this document compare with other instances of Persian tolerance in the historical record?

7.2 Herodotus, *Histories*, ca. 420s BCE

Having failed to defeat the Athenians in their first attempt in 490 BCE, the Persians launched a massive invasion of the entire Greek peninsula in 480, under the leadership of Darius's successor, Xerxes. Thirty-one Greek cities agreed to band together to resist this force of (according to Herodotus) 1,700,000 Persian soldiers, in addition to a sizeable naval contingent, Herodotus envisions a conversation between Xerxes and the Spartan defector Demaratus shortly before the first major confrontation between Persia and the Greeks at Thermopylae. In answer to the king's question, Demaratus claims that the Greeks will prove more difficult to defeat than Xerxes expects.

Having sailed from one end to the other of the line of anchored ships, Xerxes went ashore again and sent for Demaratus, the son of Ariston, who was accompanying him in the march to Greece. "Demaratus," he said, "it would give me pleasure at this point to put to you a few questions. You are a Greek, and a native, moreover, of by no means the meanest or weakest city in that country—as I learn not only from yourself but from the other Greeks I have spoken with. Tell me, then—will the Greeks dare to lift a hand against me? My own belief is that all the Greeks and all the other western peoples gathered together would be insufficient to withstand the attack of my army—and still more so if they are not united. But it is your opinion upon this subject that I should like to hear."

. . .

"I think highly," [Demaratus said,] "of all Greeks of the Dorian lands, but what I am about to say will apply not to all Dorians, but to the Spartans only. First then, they will not under any circumstances accept terms from you which would mean slavery for Greece; secondly, they will fight you even if the rest of Greece submits. Moreover, there is no use in asking if their numbers are adequate to enable them to do this; suppose a thousand of them take the field—then that thousand will fight you; and so will any number, greater than this or less."

Xerxes laughed. "Demaratus," he exclaimed, "what an extraordinary thing to say! Do you really suppose a thousand men would fight an army like mine?"

. . .

"King," Demaratus answered, "I knew before I began that if I spoke the truth you would not like it. But, as you demanded the plain truth and nothing less, I told you how things are with the Spartans. Yet you are well aware that I now feel but little affection for my countrymen, who robbed me of my hereditary power and privileges and made me a fugitive without a home—whereas your father welcomed me at his court and gave me the means of livelihood and somewhere to live. Surely it is unreasonable to reject kindness; any sensible man will cherish it. Personally I do not claim to be able to fight ten men—or two; indeed I should prefer not even to fight with one. But should it be necessary—should there be some great cause to

Source: Herodotus, *The Histories*, trans. Aubrey de Sélincourt (Harmondsworth, UK: Penguin, 1954), 403–405.

urge me on—then nothing would give me more pleasure than to stand up to one of those men of yours who claim to be a match for three Greeks. So it is with the Spartans; fighting singly, they are as good as any, but fighting together they are the best soldiers in the world. They are free—yes—but not entirely free; for they have a master, and that master is Law, which they fear much more than your subjects fear you. Whatever this master commands, they do; and his command never varies: it is never to retreat in battle, however great the odds, but always to remain in formation, and to conquer or die. If, my lord, you think that what I have said is nonsense—very well; I am willing henceforward to hold my tongue. This time I spoke because you forced me to speak. In any case, I pray that all may turn out as you desire."

Xerxes burst out laughing at Demaratus' answer, and good-humoredly let him go.

WORKING WITH SOURCES

1. For what reasons does Demaratus think the Spartans will fight so hard to resist Xerxes?
2. What does the passage reveal concerning Herodotus's attitude toward the Greeks—and the Persians?

7.3 1 Maccabees, ca. 134 BCE

Just before his death in Babylon in June 323 BCE, Alexander the Great was the unrivalled conqueror of an enormous portion of the known world, counting modern Greece, Egypt, the Middle East, Iran, and Afghanistan among his possessions. However, when he died, leaving his kingdom "to the strongest," conflicts immediately broke out among his Macedonian successors to determine who that strongest man was. A part of the military and political struggle that followed was an attempt to Hellenize, with varying levels of success, the older and more entrenched cultures Alexander had defeated as he raced through Africa and Asia. This process continued for the next three centuries, and, in the mid-second century BCE, one of these successor kings, Antiochus IV Epiphanes, attempted a brutal imposition of Greek cultural values on the Jews in Jerusalem. This effort, and the revolt it triggered, is described in the apocryphal (i.e., not part of the standard canon) Jewish book of 1 Maccabees. Notice that the Hellenistic era did not appear to everyone to have been a fortuitous blending of disparate cultures.

1 After Alexander son of Philip, the Macedonian,
who came from the land of Kittim, had defeated King
Darius of the Persians and the Medes, he succeeded
him as king. (He had previously become king of
Greece.) **2** He fought many battles, conquered strong-
holds, and put to death the kings of the earth. **3** He
advanced to the ends of the earth, and plundered
many nations. When the earth became quiet before
him, he was exalted, and his heart was lifted up. **4** He
gathered a very strong army and ruled over countries,
nations, and princes, and they became tributary to
him. **5** After this he fell sick and perceived that he was
dying. **6** So he summoned his most honored officers,
who had been brought up with him from youth, and
divided his kingdom among them while he was still
alive. **7** And after Alexander had reigned twelve years,

Source: The Apocrypha: Revised Standard Version of the Old Testament (New York: Thomas Nelson & Sons, 1957), 190–192.

he died. **8** Then his officers began to rule, each in his own place. **9** They all put on crowns after his death, and so did their descendants after them for many years; and they caused many evils on the earth.

10 From them came forth a sinful root, Antiochus Epiphanes, son of King Antiochus; he had been a hostage in Rome. He began to reign in the one hundred thirty-seventh year of the kingdom of the Greeks. **11** In those days certain renegades came out from Israel and misled many, saying, "Let us go and make a covenant with the Gentiles around us, for since we separated from them many disasters have come upon us." **12** This proposal pleased them, **13** and some of the people eagerly went to the king, who authorized them to observe the ordinances of the Gentiles. **14** So they built a gymnasium in Jerusalem, according to Gentile custom, **15** and removed the marks of circumcision, and abandoned the holy covenant. They joined with the Gentiles and sold themselves to do evil. **16** When Antiochus saw that his kingdom was established, he determined to become king of the land of Egypt, in order that he might reign over both kingdoms. **17** So he invaded Egypt with a strong force, with chariots and elephants and cavalry and with a large fleet. **18** He engaged King Ptolemy of Egypt in battle, and Ptolemy turned and fled before him, and many were wounded and fell. **19** They captured the fortified cities in the land of Egypt, and he plundered the land of Egypt.

20 After subduing Egypt, Antiochus returned in the one hundred forty-third year. He went up against Israel and came to Jerusalem with a strong force. **21** He arrogantly entered the sanctuary and took the golden altar, the lampstand for the light, and all its utensils. **22** He took also the table for the bread of the Presence, the cups for drink offerings, the bowls, the golden censers, the curtain, the crowns, and the gold decoration on the front of the temple; he stripped it all off. **23** He took the silver and the gold, and the costly vessels; he took also the hidden treasures that he found. **24** Taking them all, he went into his own land. He shed much blood, and spoke with great arrogance. **25** Israel mourned deeply in every community, **26** rulers and elders groaned, young women and young men became faint, the beauty of the women faded. **27** Every bridegroom took up the lament; she who sat in the bridal chamber was mourning. **28** Even the land trembled for its inhabitants, and all the house of Jacob was clothed with shame. **29** Two years later the king sent to the cities of Judah a chief collector of tribute, and he came to Jerusalem with a large force. **30** Deceitfully he spoke peaceable words to them, and they believed him; but he suddenly fell upon the city, dealt it a severe blow, and destroyed many people of Israel. **31** He plundered the city, burned it with fire, and tore down its houses and its surrounding walls. **32** They took captive the women and children, and seized the livestock. **33** Then they fortified the city of David with a great strong wall and strong towers, and it became their citadel.

. . .

44 And the king sent letters by messengers to Jerusalem and the towns of Judah; he directed them to follow customs strange to the land, **45** to forbid burnt offerings and sacrifices and drink offerings in the sanctuary, to profane sabbaths and festivals, **46** to defile the sanctuary and the priests, **47** to build altars and sacred precincts and shrines for idols, to sacrifice swine and other unclean animals, **48** and to leave their sons uncircumcised. They were to make themselves abominable by everything unclean and profane, **49** so that they would forget the law and change all the ordinances. **50** He added, "And whoever does not obey the command of the king shall die." **51** In such words he wrote to his whole kingdom. He appointed inspectors over all the people and commanded the towns of Judah to offer sacrifice, town by town. **52** Many of the people, everyone who forsook the law, joined them, and they did evil in the land; **53** they drove Israel into hiding in every place of refuge they had. **54** Now on the fifteenth day of Chislev, in the one hundred forty-fifth year, they erected a desolating sacrilege on the altar of burnt offering. They also built altars in the surrounding towns of Judah, **55** and offered incense at the doors of the houses and in the streets. **56** The books of the law that they found they tore to pieces and burned with fire. **57** Anyone found possessing the book of the covenant, or anyone who adhered to the law, was condemned to death by decree of the king. **58** They kept using violence against Israel, against those who were found month after month in the towns. **59** On the twenty-fifth day of the month they offered sacrifice on the altar that was on top of the altar of burnt offering. **60** According to the decree, they put to death the women who had their children circumcised, **61** and their families and those who circumcised them; and they hung the infants from their mothers' necks. **62** But many in Israel stood firm and were resolved in their hearts not to eat unclean food. **63** They chose to die rather than to be defiled by food or to profane the holy covenant; and they did die.

WORKING WITH SOURCES

1. To what specific innovations does the writer of this document object? Why?
2. What evidence is contained in this document of cultural misunderstanding?

7.4 Graffiti from the Walls of Pompeii, ca. 79 CE

This is a small sample of the array of painted, scratched, and scribbled graffiti archaeologists have discovered on the walls of the city of Pompeii, which was sealed in ash after the eruption of Mount Vesuvius in 79 CE.

I

Twenty pairs of gladiators of Decimus Lucretius Satrius Valens, life-time flamen [priest] of Nero son of Caesar Augustus [Claudius], and ten pairs of gladiators of Decimus Lucretius Valens, his son, will fight at Pompeii on April 8, 9, 10, 11, and 12. There will be a full card of wild beast combats, and awnings [for the spectators]. Aemilius Celer [painted this sign], all alone in the moonlight.

II

Market days: Saturday in Pompeii, Sunday in Nuceria, Monday in Atella, Tuesday in Nola, Wednesday in Cumae, Thursday in Puteoli, Friday in Rome.

III

6th: cheese 1, bread 8, oil 3, wine 3 [expenses in food, in coins called *asses*]

7th: bread 8, oil 5, onions 5, bowl 1, bread for the slave [?] 2, wine 2

8th: bread 8, bread for the slave [?] 4, grits 3

9th: wine for the winner 1 *denarius* [a higher denomination of coin], bread 8, wine 2, cheese 2

10th: [. . .] 1 *denarius*, bread 2, for women 8, wheat 1 *denarius*, cucumber 1, dates 1, incense 1, cheese 2, sausage 1, soft cheese 4, oil 7

IV

Pleasure says: "You can get a drink here for an *as*, a better drink for two, Falernian [fine quality wine] for four."

V

A copper pot is missing from this shop. 65 sesterces reward if anybody brings it back, 20 sesterces if he reveals the thief so we can get our property back.

VI

The weaver Successus loves the innkeeper's slave girl, Iris by name. She doesn't care for him, but he begs her to take pity on him. Written by his rival. So long.

Source: Naphtali Lewis and Meyer Reinhold, eds., *Roman Civilization: Selected Readings*, vol. 2 (New York: Columbia University Press, 1990), 276–278.

[Answer by the rival:] Just because you're bursting with envy, don't pick on a handsomer man, a lady-killer and a gallant.

[Answer by the first writer:] There's nothing more to say or write. You love Iris, and she doesn't care for you.

VII

Take your lewd looks and flirting eyes off another man's wife, and show some decency on your face!

VIII

Anybody in love, come here. I want to break Venus' ribs with a club and cripple the goddess' loins. If she can pierce my tender breast, why can't I break her head with a club?

IX

I write at Love's dictation and Cupid's instruction;
But damn it! I don't want to be a god without you.

X

[A prostitute's sign:] I am yours for 2 *asses* cash.

WORKING WITH SOURCES

1. Are you surprised by what these graffiti reveal about daily life in Pompeii?
2. How could this material be used to assess the relative standing of women in Roman society? Should it be used in this way?

7.5 The Murder of the Philosopher Hypatia, Alexandria, Egypt, ca. 415 CE

Born around 360 CE and instructed by her father, Theon, a mathematician and the last librarian of the famous Library of Alexandria, Hypatia directed the Platonic school in the city, teaching students who were of mixed religious commitments but were, presumably, all men. The few sources that mention her agree that she was abducted, stripped of her clothes, and stoned to death with roof tiles by a fanatical group of Christians, but the precise sequence of events that led to this atrocity has always been controversial.

Because all of these sources were composed by Christians—with the exception of her own correspondence with a former student, the bishop Synesius of Cyrene—the lynching of Hypatia may be interpreted as an instance of fanaticism attempting to destroy reason, or as the elimination of a dangerous pagan influence in the midst of a Christianizing Egypt. The latter approach has, unfortunately, been more common, given Christian influence—and misogyny—in Western societies and the installation of her main opponent, Bishop Cyril of Alexandria, as one of the "Fathers of the Church."

Source: Socrates, *Ecclesiastical History* 7.15, available online at http://www.stoa.org/diotima/anthology/wlgr/wlgr-religion451.shtml.

There was a woman in Alexandria named Hypatia. She was the daughter of the philosopher Theon. She had progressed so far in her education that she surpassed by far the philosophers of her time, and took over the Neoplatonic school that derived from Plotinus, and set forth every philosophical approach to those who wanted to learn them. Accordingly people from all over who wanted to study philosophy rushed to her side. Because of the dignified reputation that derived from her education, she began (with due modesty) to address even the rulers. And she had no hesitation about being in the company of men, since they all respected her more because of her extraordinary chastity.

Then she became the subject of envy. Because she was frequently in the company of Orestes, people in the church began to slander her, as if that were what was preventing Orestes from making friends with the bishop. Some hot-headed men who agreed with this, who were led by a certain Peter the Reader, were on the lookout for the woman when she returned to her house from wherever she had been. They threw her out of her carriage, and dragged her to the church known as Caesarion. They tore off her clothing, and killed her with potsherds. When they had torn her apart limb from limb, they took the pieces of her body to the place called Cinaron, and burned them.

This act did no small amount of damage to Cyril and to the Church at Alexandria. For murder and fighting, and everything of that sort, are totally alien to those who believe in Christ. These events took place after Cyril had been bishop for four years, and Theodosius for ten [c. 415 CE], in the month of March, during Lent.

. . .

About Hypatia the philosopher. An illustration of how disorderly the Alexandrians are. She was born and raised and educated in Alexandria. She inherited her father's extraordinarily distinguished nature, and was not satisfied with the training in mathematics that she received from her father, but turned to other learning also in a distinguished way. Although she was a woman she put on a man's cloak and made her way into the center of the city and gave to those who wanted to listen public lectures about Plato or Aristotle or about some other philosophers. In addition to her teaching she also excelled in the practical arts, being just and chaste, she remained a virgin, though she was so beautiful to look at that one of her pupils fell in love with her. When he was no longer able to control his passion, he let her know how he felt about her. The uneducated stories have it that Hypatia told him to cure his disease through the study of the arts. But the truth is that he had long since given up on culture; instead, she brought in one of those women's rags and threw it at him, revealing her unclean nature, and said to him, "This is what you are in love with, young man, and not with the Beautiful," and in shame and wonder at this ugly display his soul was converted and he became more chaste.

That (according to this account) is what Hypatia was like, skilled in debate and dialectic, intelligent in her conduct and politically adept. The other citizens understandably were fond of her and accorded her the greatest respect, and the current magistrates of the town always went first to her, as used to happen also in Athens. For even though the practice had died out, the name of philosophy still seemed distinguished and impressive to the people who had primary charge of the city. It then happened that the man in charge of the opposing sect, Cyril, passed by Hypatia's house and saw a large crowd in front of the door, consisting of men and horses, some arriving, some leaving, and some waiting there. He asked what the gathering was, and why there was commotion in front of the house, and learned from his followers that the philosopher Hypatia was giving a lecture and that this was her house. And when he learned this he was very upset and soon planned her murder, the most unholy of all murders. As she was going out to lecture, as was her custom, a group of bestial men attacked her, true ruffians, who had no respect for God and no concern for men's indignation; they killed the philosopher and brought the greatest pollution and disgrace on their fatherland.

WORKING WITH SOURCES

1. Was Hypatia killed principally because she was a female philosopher or because she was a non-Christian philosopher?
2. How did Hypatia both refer to and transcend the boundaries placed upon women in ancient Greco-Roman society?

8. EMPIRES AND VISIONARIES IN INDIA, 600 BCE–600 CE

8.1 The Seven Pillar Edicts of King Ashoka, ca. 247–246 BCE

The third of the Mauryan kings, Ashoka ruled a vast empire throughout the Indian subcontinent in the period 273–231 BCE. His abrupt conversion to Buddhism in 260 led him to govern according to Buddhist principles—at least as he understood them. His new policies with respect to "righteous" governance were posted in a series of edicts that were engraved on rocks and pillars at strategic spots in his empire. A sample of these contains both very specific injunctions—imposed upon himself and upon his subordinates—and general principles, which could presumably be adapted to changing real-world circumstances?

1 Beloved-of-the-Gods speaks thus: This Dharma edict was written twenty-six years after my coronation. Happiness in this world and the next is difficult to obtain without much love for the Dharma, much self-examination, much respect, much fear (of evil), and much enthusiasm. But through my instruction this regard for Dharma and love of Dharma has grown day by day, and will continue to grow. And my officers of high, low and middle rank are practicing and conforming to Dharma, and are capable of inspiring others to do the same. Mahamatras in border areas are doing the same. And these are my instructions: to protect with Dharma, to make happiness through Dharma and to guard with Dharma.

. . .

4 Beloved-of-the-Gods speaks thus: This Dharma edict was written twenty-six years after my coronation. My Rajjukas are working among the people, among many hundreds of thousands of people. The hearing of petitions and the administration of justice has been left to them so that they can do their duties confidently and fearlessly and so that they can work for the welfare, happiness and benefit of the people in the country. But they should remember what causes happiness and sorrow, and being themselves devoted to Dharma, they should encourage the people in the country (to do the same), that they may attain happiness in this world and the next. These Rajjukas are eager to serve me. They also obey other officers who know my desires, who instruct the Rajjukas so that they can please me. Just as a person feels confident having entrusted his child to an expert nurse thinking: "The nurse will keep my child well," even so, the Rajjukas have been appointed by me for the welfare and happiness of the people in the country.

The hearing of petitions and the administration of justice have been left to the Rajjukas so that they can do their duties unperturbed, fearlessly and confidently. It is my desire that there should be uniformity in law and uniformity in sentencing. I even go this far, to grant a three-day stay for those in prison who have been tried and sentenced to death. During this time

Source: Ven. S. Dhammika, trans. DharmaNet, 1994, http://www.cs.colostate.edu/~malaiya/ashoka.html#PILLAR.

their relatives can make appeals to have the prisoners' lives spared. If there is none to appeal on their behalf, the prisoners can give gifts in order to make merit for the next world, or observe fasts. Indeed, it is my wish that in this way, even if a prisoner's time is limited, he can prepare for the next world, and that people's Dharma practice, self-control and generosity may grow.

7 Beloved-of-the-Gods, King Piyadasi, says: Along roads I have had banyan trees planted so that they can give shade to animals and men, and I have had mango groves planted. At intervals of eight **krosas**, I have had wells dug, rest-houses built, and in various places, I have had watering-places made for the use of animals and men. But these are but minor achievements. Such things to make the people happy have been done by former kings. I have done these things for this purpose, that the people might practice the Dharma.

Beloved-of-the-Gods, King Piyadasi, speaks thus: My Dharma Mahamatras too are occupied with various good works among the ascetics and householders of all religions. I have ordered that they should be occupied with the affairs of the Sangha. I have also ordered that they should be occupied with the affairs of the Brahmans and the Ajivikas. I have ordered that they be occupied with the Niganthas. In fact, I have ordered that different Mahamatras be occupied with the particular affairs of all different religions. And my Dharma Mahamatras likewise are occupied with these and other religions.

Beloved-of-the-Gods, King Piyadasi, speaks thus: These and other principal officers are occupied with the distribution of gifts, mine as well as those of the queens. In my women's quarters, they organize various charitable activities here and in the provinces. I have also ordered my sons and the sons of other queens to distribute gifts so that noble deeds of Dharma and the practice of Dharma may be promoted. And noble deeds of Dharma and the practice of Dharma consist of having kindness, generosity, truthfulness, purity, gentleness and goodness increase among the people.

Beloved-of-the-Gods, King Piyadasi, speaks thus: Whatever good deeds have been done by me, those the people accept and those they follow. Therefore they have progressed and will continue to progress by being respectful to mother and father, respectful to elders, by courtesy to the aged and proper behavior towards Brahmans and ascetics, towards the poor and distressed, and even towards servants and employees.

Beloved-of-the-Gods, King Piyadasi, speaks thus: This progress among the people through Dharma has been done by two means, by Dharma regulations and by persuasion. Of these, Dharma regulation is of little effect, while persuasion has much more effect. The Dharma regulations I have given are that various animals must be protected. And I have given many other Dharma regulations also. But it is by persuasion that progress among the people through Dharma has had a greater effect in respect of harmlessness to living beings and non-killing of living beings.

Krosas: Unit of land measure.

WORKING WITH SOURCES

1. To what extent did Ashoka claim to be occupying a paternal role in relationship to his people? Is it likely his specific instructions were actually carried out?
2. Are there indications here that Ashoka really aimed at creating what we might perceive as a kind of police state? In what respects?

8.2 *The Questions of King Milinda (The Milindapanha),* ca. 100 BCE

A series of Greek rulers attempted to maintain the Hellenizing goals of Alexander the Great in Bactria (modern Afghanistan), long after his death in 323 BCE. The most famous ruler in this line was Menander I (ca. 160–130 BCE), who achieved immortality in Buddhist literature by engaging in a debate with the Buddhist sage Nagasena. Their talks, set out as a series of dilemmas to be posed and (if possible) resolved, became an important exposition of Buddhist ideas and supposedly led to the conversion of Menander ("King Milinda") to Buddhism. In any event, *The Milindapanha* reflects the fusion of Greek and Indian traditions of philosophy, in the fascinating cauldron of world contact that existed in Central and South Asia.

DILEMMA THE FORTY-SECOND. MODERATION IN FOOD

4 'Venerable Nâgasena, the Blessed One said:

"Be not remiss as to (the rules to be observed) when standing up (to beg for food). Be restrained in (matters relating to) the stomach."

But on the other hand he said:

"Now there were several days, Udâyin, on which I ate out of this bowl when it was full to the brim, and ate even more."

"Now if the first rule be true, then the second statement must be false. But if the statement be true, then the rule first quoted must be wrong.

This too is a double-edged problem, now put to you, which you have to solve."

5 . . . He who has no self-control as regards the stomach, O king, will destroy living creatures, will take possession of what has not been given to him, will be unchaste, will speak lies, will drink strong drink, will put his mother or his father to death, will slay an Arahat, will create a schism in the Order, will even with malice aforethought wound a Tathâgata. Was it not, O king, when without restraint as to his stomach, that Devadatta by breaking up the Order, heaped up for himself karma that would endure for a kalpa? It was on calling to mind this, O king, and many other things of the same kind, that the Blessed One declared:

Be not remiss as to (the rules to be observed) when standing up (to beg for food). Be restrained in (matters relating to) the stomach."

6 'And he who has self-control as regards the stomach gains a clear insight into the Four Truths, realizes the Four Fruits of the life of renunciation, and attains to mastery over the Four Discriminations, the Eight Attainments, and the Six Modes of Higher Knowledge, and fulfils all that goes to constitute the life of the recluse. Did not the parrot fledgling, O king, by self-restraint as to his stomach, cause the very heaven of the great Thirty-Three to shake, and bring down Sakka, the king of the gods, to wait upon him? It was on calling to mind this, O king, and many other things of a similar kind, that the Blessed One declared:

"Be not remiss as to (the rules to be observed) when standing up (to beg for food). Be restrained in (matters relating to) the stomach."

7 'But when, O king, the Blessed One said: "Now there were several days, Udâyi, on which I ate out of this bowl when it was full to the brim, and ate even more," that was said by him who had completed his task, who had finished all that he had to do, who had

Source: The Questions of King Milinda, trans. T. W. Rhys Davids, vol. 2 (Oxford: Clarendon, 1894), 4–7 and 20–22.

accomplished the end he set before him, who had overcome every obstruction, by the self-dependent Tathâgata himself about himself.

Just, O king, as it is desirable that a sick man to whom an emetic, or a purge, or a clyster has been administered, should be treated with a tonic; just so, O king, should the man who is full of evil, and who has not perceived the Four Truths, adopt the practice of restraint in the matter of eating. But just, O king, as there is no necessity of polishing, and rubbing down, and purifying a diamond gem of great brilliancy, of the finest water, and of natural purity; just so, O king, is there no restraint as to what actions he should perform, on the Tathâgata, on him who hath attained to perfection in all that lies within the scope of a Buddha.'

'Very good, Nâgasena! That is so, and I accept it as you say.'

. . .

DILEMMA THE FORTY-SIXTH. THE MOCKING OF THE BUDDHA

19 'Venerable Nâgasena, it was said by the Blessed One of Six-tusks, the elephant king,

"When he sought to slay him, and had reached him with his trunk,
He perceived the yellow robe, the badge of a recluse,
Then, though smarting with the pain, the thought possessed his heart,—
'He who wears the outward garb the Arahats wear
Must be scatheless held, and sacred, by the good.'"

'But on the other hand it is said:

"When he was Gotipâla, the young Brahman, he reviled and abused Kassapa the Blessed One, the Arahat, the Buddha supreme, with vile and bitter words, calling him a shaveling and a good-for-nothing monk."

'Now if, Nâgasena, the Bodisat, even when he was an animal, respected the yellow robe, then the statement that as Gotipâla, a Brahman, he reviled and abused the Blessed One of that time, must be false. But if as a Brahman, he reviled and abused the Blessed One, the statement that when he was Six-tusks, the elephant king, he respected the yellow robe, must be false. If when the Bodisat was an animal, though he was suffering severe and cruel and bitter pain, he respected the yellow robe which the hunter had put on, how was it that when he was a man, a man arrived at discretion, with all his knowledge mature, he did not pay reverence, on seeing him, to Kassapa the Blessed One, the Arahat, the Buddha supreme, one endowed with the ten powers, the leader of the world, the highest of the high, round whom effulgence spread a fathom on every side, and who was clad in most excellent and precious and delicate Benares cloth made into yellow robes? This too is a double-edged problem, now put to you, which you have to solve.'

20 'The verse you have quoted, O king, was spoken by the Blessed One. And Kassapa the Blessed One, the Arahat, the Buddha supreme, was abused and reviled by Gotipâla the young Brahman with vile and bitter words, with the epithets of shaveling and good-for-nothing monk. But that was owing to his birth and family surroundings. For Gotipâla, O king, was descended from a family of unbelievers, men void of faith. His mother and father, his sisters and brothers, the bondswomen and bondsmen, the hired servants and dependents in the house, were worshippers of Brahmâ, reverers of Brahmâ; and harboring the idea that Brahmans were the highest and most honorable among men, they reviled and loathed those others who had renounced the world. It was through hearing what they said that Gotipâla, when invited by Ghatîkâra the potter to visit the teacher, replied: "What's the good to you of visiting that shaveling, that good-for-nothing monk?"

21 'Just, O king, as even nectar when mixed with poison will turn sour, just as the coolest water in contact with fire will become warm, so was it that Gotipâla, the young Brahman, having been born and brought up in a family of unbelievers, men void of faith, thus reviled and abused the Tathâgata after the manner of his kind. And just, O king, as a flaming and burning mighty fire, if, even when at the height of its glory, it should come into contact with water, would cool down, with its splendor and glory spoilt, and turn to cinders, black as rotten blighted fruits—just so, O king, Gotipâla, full as he was of merit and faith, mighty as was the glory of his knowledge, yet when reborn into a family of unbelievers, of men void of faith, he became, as it were, blind, and reviled and abused the Tathâgata. But when he had gone to him, and had come to know the virtues of the Buddhas which he had, then did he become as his hired servant; and having renounced the world and entered the Order under the system of the Conqueror, he gained the fivefold power of insight, and the eightfold power of ecstatic meditation, and became assured of rebirth into the Brahmâ heaven.'

'Very good, Nâgasena! That is so, and I accept it as you say.'

WORKING WITH SOURCES

1. To what extent does this dialogue reflect elements of the Greek philosophical tradition, explored in Chapter 7?
2. How do both speakers deploy real-world examples, in order to enhance their philosophical arguments?

8.3 Bamiyan Buddhas, Afghanistan, Late Sixth Century CE

A few months before the 9/11 terrorist attacks, in the spring of 2001, Taliban officials oversaw a series of explosions in the Bamiyan Valley, which deliberately detonated priceless elements of world heritage. Among the victims of this depredation were a set of enormous Buddha statues that had symbolized the unity of peoples in the region across religious lines. The two statues of Buddha (at 35 and 53 meters in height, one was the tallest Buddha in the world until its destruction) were rendered in a blended Hellenistic and South Asian style. Even after the collapse of the Taliban regime in Afghanistan, little has been done to restore the objects. (Left: an 1880 drawing showing how they originally appeared; right: what remained of the statues after their destruction.)

Source: © SuperStock (left); © Graciela Gonzalez Brigas (right).

WORKING WITH SOURCES

1. Why and under what circumstances would Buddhas have been carved into this mountainside in the first place?
2. Can any monotheistic system tolerate a fusion of cultural and religious values?

8.4 Seated Buddha, from the Gandhara Culture, Afghanistan-Pakistan, Second–Third Centuries CE

Gandhara became the center of a vibrant artistic tradition for several centuries. As Greek Bactrians merged their cultural values with Buddhists, Hellenistic artistic techniques fused with the practices of Mahayana Buddhism, yielding a renaissance of daring, boldly innovative sculpture. Among the products of this cultural synthesis was a seated Buddha which incorporates both Hellenistic and Indian aesthetic elements.

Source:

WORKING WITH SOURCES

1. In what specific respects does this object reflect a conflation of Greek and Indian imagery, especially in the styles of clothing and hair?
2. Why is this object in the British Museum in London today?

8.5 Kalidasa, *The Cloud Messenger*, ca. Fourth–Fifth Centuries CE

Sometimes described as the "Shakespeare of India," Kalidasa mastered various literary genres in his lifetime and continued to thrive, even in Western translations, into modern times. He composed three plays, two epic poems, and a series of shorter poems. Among these is *The Cloud Messenger*, in which a man asks a passing cloud to carry a message to his beloved wife, who is awaiting him in the Himalayas. Translated from the Sanskrit into English in the early nineteenth century, *The Cloud Messenger* served as the inspiration for composer Gustav Holst's 1909–1910 choral work *The Cloud Messenger*.

Source: http://allpoetry.com/poem/8526541-The-Cloud-Messenger---Part-01-by-Kalidasa

A certain **yaksha** who had been negligent in the execution of his own duties, on account of a curse from his master which was to be endured for a year and which was onerous as it separated him from his beloved, made his residence among the hermitages of Ramagiri, whose waters were blessed by the bathing of the daughter of Janaka and whose shade trees grew in profusion.

That lover, separated from his beloved, whose gold armlet had slipped from his bare forearm, having dwelt on that mountain for some months, on the first day of the month of Asadha, saw a cloud embracing the summit, which resembled a mature elephant playfully butting a bank.

Managing with difficulty to stand up in front of that cloud which was the cause of the renewal of his enthusiasm, that attendant of the king of kings, pondered while holding back his tears. Even the mind of a happy person is excited at the sight of a cloud. How much more so, when the one who longs to cling to his neck is far away?

As the month of Nabhas was close at hand, having as his goal the sustaining of the life of his beloved and wishing to cause the tidings of his own welfare to be carried by the cloud, the delighted being spoke kind words of welcome to the cloud to which offerings of fresh kutaja flowers had been made.

Owing to his impatience, not considering the incompatibility between a cloud consisting of vapor, light, water and wind and the contents of his message best delivered by a person of normal faculties, the yaksha made this request to the cloud, for among sentient and non-sentient things, those afflicted by desire are naturally miserable:

Without doubt, your path unimpeded, you will see your brother's wife, intent on counting the days, faithful and living on. The bond of hope generally sustains the quickly sinking hearts of women who are alone, and which wilt like flowers.

Just as the favorable wind drives you slowly onward, this cataka cuckoo, your kinsman, calls sweetly on the left. Knowing the season for fertilization, cranes, like threaded garlands in the sky, lovely to the eye, will serve you.

Your steady passage observed by charming female **siddhas** who in trepidation wonder 'Has the summit been carried off the mountain by the wind?,' you who are heading north, fly up into the sky from this place where the nicula trees flourish, avoiding on the way the blows of the trunks of the elephants of the four quarters of the sky. . . .

Even though the route would be circuitous for one who, like you, is northward-bound, do not turn your back on the love on the palace roofs in Ujjayini. If you do not enjoy the eyes with flickering eyelids of the women startled by bolts of lightning there, then you have been deceived!

On the way, after you have ascended to the Nirvandhya River, whose girdles are flocks of birds calling on account of the turbulence of her waves, whose gliding motion is rendered delightful with stumbling steps, and whose exposed navel is her eddies, fill yourself with water, for amorous distraction is a woman's first expression of love for their beloved.

When you have passed that, you should duly adopt the means by which the Sindhu River may cast off her emaciation—she whose waters have become like a single braid of hair, whose complexion is made pale by the old leaves falling from the trees on her banks, and who shows you goodwill because she has been separated from you, O fortunate one.

. . .

Even if you arrive at Mahakala at some other time, O cloud, you should wait until the sun passes

---

Yaksha: A demigod attendant to the god of wealth.

Siddhas: Experts in spiritual matters.

from the range of the eye. Playing the honorable role of drum at the evening offering to Shiva, you will receive the full reward for your deep thunder.

There, their girdles jingling to their footsteps, and their hands tired from the pretty waving of fly-whisks whose handles are brilliant with the sparkle of jewels, having received from you raindrops at the onset of the rainy season that soothe the scratches made by fingernails, the courtesans cast you lingering side-long glances that resemble rows of honey-bees.

Then, settled above the forests whose trees are like uplifted arms, being round in shape, producing an evening light, red as a fresh China-rose, at the start of Shiva's dance, remove his desire for a fresh elephant skin—you whose devotion is beheld by Parvati, her agitation stilled and her gaze transfixed.

WORKING WITH SOURCES

1. How do the places seen by the cloud on its journey relate to the husband's feeling of longing for his wife?
2. How are the outer and inner worlds connected in this poem?

9. CHINA: IMPERIAL UNIFICATION AND PERFECTING THE MORAL ORDER, 722 BCE–618 CE

9.1 *Analects* (*Lunyu*) of Confucius, ca. 500–479 BCE

The details of Confucius's life are murky, especially given the chaos surrounding the declining Zhou period in the 490s and 480s BCE. It is important to take into account the impact of interstate conflict on Confucius's philosophical insights. A commoner who was effectively shut out of power by the three noble clans of Lu, Confucius was eventually driven out and forced to wander among the other states, due to the resentment of this traditional aristocracy. Despite the resistance of warring aristocrats, Confucius advocated a new approach to government, in which respect for the weak, poor, and defenseless would form the basis for civil society.

[12.7] Zigong asked about government. The Master [Confucius] said, "Sufficient food, sufficient arms, and popular trust [in the ruler]."

Zigong said, "If this were impossible, and we would have to dispense with one of these three, which should come first?"

[Confucius] said, "Dispense with arms."

Zigong said, "If this were impossible, and we would have to dispense with one of these two, which should come first?"

[Confucius] said, "Dispense with food. Since antiquity, there has always been death. But people without trust have no standing."

[12.11] Lord Jing of Qi asked Confucius about government. Confucius answered, "The lord acts as a lord, the minister, the father as a father, the son as a son."

The lord said, "Excellent! Surely, if the lord does not act as a lord, nor the minister as a minister, nor the father as a father, nor the son as a son, then although I might have grain, would I be able to eat it?"

[12.13] The Master said, "In hearing litigation, I am like other people. What is necessary is to cause there to be no litigation."

[12.17] Ji Kangzi asked Confucius about government. Confucius answered, "To govern is to correct. If you lead with rectitude, who will dare not be correct?"

[12.18] Ji Kangzi was vexed at the thieving [in his state] and asked Confucius about it. Confucius answered, "If you, sir, were not covetous, then even if you were to reward them for it, they would not steal."

[13.3] Zilu said, "The Lord of Wei is waiting for you to effect government. What will you do first?"

The Master said, "What is necessary is to rectify names!"

Zilu said, "Is there such a thing? Master, you are wide of the mark. Why such rectification?"

The Master said, "You, you are uncouth. A noble man should appear more reserved about what he does not know. If names are not rectified, then speech

Source: Victor H. Mair, Nancy Shatzman Steinhardt, and Paul R. Goldin, eds., *Hawai'i Reader in Traditional Chinese Culture* (Honolulu: University of Hawai'i Press, 2005), 48–49.

does not flow properly. If speech does not flow properly, then affairs are not completed. If affairs are not completed, then ritual and music do not flourish. If ritual and music do not flourish, then punishments and penalties do not hit the mark. If punishments and penalties do not hit the mark, the people have no way to move hand or foot. Thus, for the noble man, names must be able to be spoken, and what he speaks must be able to be carried out. With regard to his speech, the noble man's [concern] is simply that there be nothing that is careless."

[13.10] The Master said, "If there were one [among the princes] who would make use of me, within no more than twelve months, [the government] would be acceptable. Within three years there would be success."

WORKING WITH SOURCES

1. To what extent did Confucius expect to be consulted by the leaders of the various states?
2. What does he seem to have envisioned as the ultimate basis of proper government?

9.2 *Book of Mencius* (Mengzi), ca. 310–289 BCE

A later student of Confucian doctrine, Master Meng (ca. 371–289 BCE) spread the teachings of the master, while also making his own distinctive contributions. Having traveled throughout China spreading Confucian ideals, particularly as a basis for governmental practice, Mencius composed a book that was in more of a narrative form than the *Analects* and was supplemented by stories, parables, and debates. He often used imagery drawn from the natural world and advocated the rulers' involvement in cultivating a "well-field" system, both literally and metaphorically.

[6A.2.] Master Gao said, "Human *xing* [nature] is like a torrent of water. If you clear a passage for it to the east, it will flow to the east; if you clear a passage for it to the west, it will flow to the west. Human *xing* is not divided into good or not good, just as water is not divided into east and west."

Mencius said, "Water is indeed not divided into east and west, but is it not divided into higher and lower? The goodness of human *xing* is like water's tendency to go downward. There is no person without goodness; there is no water that does not go downward. Now as for water, if you strike it and make it leap up, you can cause it to pass over your forehead; if you dam it and make it move [in a certain direction], you can cause it to stay on a mountain. Is this the *xing* of the water? Or is it force that makes it so? When people are caused to become bad, their *xing* is also like this."

[6A.8.] Mencius said, "The trees of Ox Mountain were once beautiful. Because it was in the suburbs of a great city, with axes and hatchets chopping at it, could it remain beautiful? With the respite that [the mountain] was afforded by the nights, and the moisture of the rain and dew, it was not without buds and sprouts that grew on it; but then the cattle and goats came to pasture there. That is why it is so bald. People see its baldness and suppose that it never had timber on it. Is this the *xing* of the mountain?

"Even what exists within human beings—are we without a mind of humanity and righteousness? The

Source: Victor H. Mair, Nancy Shatzman Steinhardt, and Paul R. Goldin, eds., *Hawai'i Reader in Traditional Chinese Culture* (Honolulu: University of Hawai'i Press, 2005), 60–61.

manner in which we let go of our good minds is like axes and hatchets with respect to trees. If [the trees] are chopped down every morning, can they remain beautiful? With the respite that we are afforded by the nights, and the [restorative influence] of the morning airs, our likes and dislikes are close to those of other people. [But the power of this restorative process] is slight, and it is fettered and destroyed by what takes place during the day. When this fettering is repeated again and again, the [restorative] nocturnal airs are insufficient to preserve [our goodness]. If the nocturnal airs are insufficient to preserve [our goodness], then we are not far from being disobedient beasts. People see our bestiality, and suppose that there was never any ability in us. Is this human *xing*?

"Thus, if it obtains its nourishment, no creature will fail to grow; if it loses its nourishment, no creature will fail to decay.

"Confucius said, 'It is to the mind alone that the following refers! If you grasp it, it will be preserved; if you discard it, it will be destroyed. There is no time to its comings and goings, and no one knows its province.'"

[6A.10.] Mencius said, "Fish is what I desire; bear's paw is also what I desire. Of the two, if I cannot have both, I will set aside fish and take bear's paw. Life is what I desire; righteousness is also what I desire. Of the two, if I cannot have both, I will set aside life and take righteousness.

"Life is surely something I desire, but there are things I desire more than life, and thus I will not act improperly in order to retain [life]. Death is surely something I hate, but there are things I hate more than death, and thus there are troubles that I do not avoid.

"If one were to make people desire nothing more than life, then why would they not use every means by which they could retain their lives? If one were to make people hate nothing more than death, then why would they not do anything by which they could avoid trouble?

"There are cases where we do not use some means that would ensure our life, and there are cases where we do not do something that would ensure our avoidance of trouble.

"Therefore, there are things that we desire more than life, and there are things that we hate more than death—and it is not only a moral paragon who has such a mind. All people have it; the moral paragon is able to keep it from perishing."

WORKING WITH SOURCES

1. How does Mencius deploy naturalistic images to illustrate his points?
2. What does the parable of Ox Mountain indicate about the existence of evil people?

9.3 Li Si, "Memorial on the Burning of Books," from the *Shiji*, ca. 100 BCE

Virtually no records have survived from the period between the unification of China in 221 BCE and the collapse of the Qin Empire 15 years later. Accordingly, historians are forced to rely on documents composed during the Han dynasty for relevant information. Nevertheless, one of the stories passed along, concerning the advice of Li Si to the emperor, is a stark reminder of how fragile learning can be, even in a temporarily successful polity. The *Records of the Grand Historian* (*Shiji*), a lengthy history of China compiled by Sima Qian (ca. 145–86 BCE), also includes a detailed biography of Li Si.

Source: Shih chi 87:6b–7a, in de Bary and Bloom, comps., *Sources of Chinese Tradition*, vol. 1 (New York: Columbia University Press, 1960), 140–141.

In earlier times the empire disintegrated and fell into disorder, and no one was capable of unifying it. Thereupon the various feudal lords rose to power. In their discourses they all praised the past in order to disparage the present and embellished empty words to confuse the truth. Everyone cherished his own favorite school of learning and criticized what had been instituted by the authorities. But at present Your Majesty possesses a unified empire, has regulated the distinctions of black and white, and has firmly established for yourself a position of sole supremacy. And yet these independent schools, joining with each other, criticize the codes of laws and instructions. Hearing of the promulgation of a decree, they criticize it, each from the standpoint of his own school. At home they disapprove of it in their hearts; going out they criticize it in the thoroughfare. They seek a reputation by discrediting their sovereign; they appear superior by expressing contrary views, and they lead the lowly multitude in the spreading of slander. If such license is not prohibited, the sovereign power will decline above and partisan factions will form below. It would be well to prohibit this.

Your servant suggests that all books in the imperial archives, save the memoirs of Qin, be burned. All persons in the empire, except members of the Academy of Learned Scholars, in possession of the *Book of Odes*, the *Book of History*, and discourses of the hundred philosophers should take them to the local governors and have them indiscriminately burned. Those who dare to talk to each other about the *Book of Odes* and the *Book of History* should be executed and their bodies exposed in the market place. Anyone referring to the past to criticize the present should, together with all the members of his family, be put to death. Officials who fail to report cases that have come under their attention are equally guilty. After thirty days from the time of issuing the decree, those who have not destroyed their books are to be branded and sent to build the Great Wall. Books not to be destroyed will be those on medicine and pharmacy, divination by the tortoise and milfoil, and agriculture and arboriculture. People wishing to pursue learning should take the officials as their teachers.

WORKING WITH SOURCES

1. Li Si's advice may seem extreme, but is there a logical element to his reasoning?
2. Why was he advocating the destruction of these specific books?

9.4 *Han Shu (History of the Former Han Dynasty), ca. 100 CE*

This dynastic history was a continuation of the *Records of the Grand Historian* (*Shiji*), originally compiled by Sima Qian (ca. 145–86 BCE), and it repeats many of the phrases and situations Sima Qian had described verbatim. However, these histories provide remarkable insights into the behavior of emperors and their families at court—while also suggesting developing notions of gender and education. This segment of the *Han Shu* covers the reign of Hsiao-Ai, in roughly 6–1 BCE.

Source: Han Shu, Book 11 (Annals of the Emperor Hsiao-Ai), Chinese text and English translation: http://www2.iath.virginia.edu/saxon/servlet/SaxonServlet?source=xwomen/texts/hanshu.xml&style=xwomen/xsl/dynaxml.xsl&chunk.id=d2.49&toc.depth=1&toc.id=0&doc.lang=bilingual.

THE ANNALS OF [EMPEROR HSIAO]-AI

Emperor Hsiao-ai was the grandson of Emperor Yüan by a concubine and the son of King Kung of Ting-t'ao, [Liu K'ang(1a)]. His mother was the Concubine [née] Ting. When he was in his third year, he succeeded [his father] and was set up as King. When he grew up, he delighted in words and phrases and in the laws and statutes.

In [the period] Yüan-yen, the fourth year, he came [to Ch'ang-an] to pay court, followed by all [his high officials], his Tutor, his Chancellor, and his Commandant of the Capital. At that time the youngest brother of Emperor Ch'eng, King Hsiao of Chung-shan, [Liu Hsing], also came to pay court, followed [only] by his Tutor. The Emperor thought it strange, and asked [Liu Hsin(5), the future Emperor Ai], about it. The King of Ting-t'ao, replied, "According to the [imperial] ordinances, when vassal kings come to pay court, they are permitted to be accompanied by the [officials ranking at] two thousand piculs in their kingdoms. The Tutor, Chancellor, and Commandant of the Capital are all [officials ranking at] two thousand piculs in a kingdom, hence I am accompanied by them all." The Emperor ordered him to recite from the *Book of Odes*, and he understood and was versed in it, and was able to explain it.

On another day, [the Emperor] asked the King of Chung-shan, [Liu Hsing], in what law or ordinance [it was ordered that he should be] accompanied only by his tutor, and he was unable to reply. [The Emperor] ordered him to recite from the *Book of History*, and he broke off [in the middle of his recitation]. Moreover, [at an imperial feast], when he had been granted food in the presence of [the Emperor], he was the last to finish eating; when he arose, his stockings came down, [for] their ties had become loosened. Because of these [facts], Emperor Ch'eng considered that he was incapable, and esteemed the King of Ting-t'ao, as capable, often exalting his abilities.

At this time the grandmother of the King, the Queen Dowager [of Ting-t'ao, née] Fu, had come with the King to pay court, and privately sent presents to the Brilliant Companion [née] Chao, whom the Emperor favored, and to the Emperor's maternal uncle, the General of Agile Cavalry and Marquis of Ch'ü-yang, Wang Ken. The Brilliant Companion [née Chao] and [Wang] Ken saw that the Emperor had no sons, and also wished beforehand to attach themselves [to the coming ruler] by a plan for the distant future, so both in turn praised the King of Ting-t'ao and urged the Emperor to make him his successor. Emperor Ch'eng of his own volition also exalted [Liu Hsin(5)'s] ability, and after having put the bonnet of virility upon him, sent him [back to his kingdom]. At that time he had [reached] his seventeenth year.

. . .

In [the period] Sui-ho, the second year, the third month, Emperor Ch'eng died, and in the fourth month, on [the day] *ping-wu*, the Heir-apparent took the imperial throne and presented himself in the Temple of [Emperor] Kao. He honored the Empress Dowager [nee Wang] with the title, Grand August Empress Dowager, and the Empress [née Chao] with the title, Empress Dowager. He [granted] a general amnesty to the empire, granted one quadriga of horses to each king's son of the imperial house who was enregistered, to the officials and common people, noble ranks, to [each] hundred households, an ox and wine, and to the Thrice Venerable, the Filially Pious, the Fraternally Respectful, the [Diligent] Cultivators of the Fields, widowers, widows, orphans, and childless, silk.

The Grand Empress Dowager [nee Wang] issued an imperial edict honoring King Kung of Ting-t'ao, [Liu K'ang], as Sovereign Kung [of Ting-t'ao]. In the fifth month, on [the day] *ping-hsü*, [the Emperor] established the Empress née Fu [as Empress]. An imperial edict said, "[According to the principle of] the *Spring and Autumn*, [in the *Kung-yang Commentary*] that 'a mother becomes honorable because of her son,' [We] honor the Queen Dowager [née Fu] of Ting-t'ao with the title, Empress Dowager Kung, and the Concubine [née] Ting [of Ting-t'ao with the title, Empress Kung, and establish for each an entourage, a Supervisor of the Household, and the income of an estate, like [the occupants of] the Ch'ang-hsin Palace and the Inner Palace. [We] posthumously honor the father of [the Empress Dowager nee] Fu as the Marquis [through Whom the Emperor] Renders Homage to an Ancestor, and the father of [the Empress nee] Ting as the Marquis in Recompense to his Virtue." The maternal uncle [of the Emperor], Ting Ming, had been made the Marquis of Yang-an, his maternal uncle's son, [Ting] Man, was made Marquis of Ping-chou, and [Ting] Man's father, [Ting] Chung, was posthumously [granted] the posthumous name, Marquis Huai of P'ing-chou. The Empress [née Fu's] father, [Fu(4)] Yen, had become the Marquis of K'ung-hsiang, and the younger brother of the Empress Dowager [nee Chao], the Palace Attendant and Imperial Household Grandee Chao Ch'in(b), became the Marquis of Hsin-ch'eng.

In the sixth month, an imperial edict said, "'The melodies of Cheng are licentious' and bring disorder into music. They were banished by the Sage-kings. Let the Bureau of Music be abolished."

WORKING WITH SOURCES

1. What was thought to be the best course of education for the young Emperor?
2. What seems to have been the extent of the power of the Empress Dowager? Why?

9.5 Ban Zhao, *Admonitions for Women (Nüjie)*, ca. 80 CE

Ban Zhao (45–ca. 116 CE) was by far the most educated woman of her day, and she trained many important male scholars. The *Han Shu* (the continuation of Sima Qian's *Shiji*) was originally undertaken by her father, Ban Biao (3–54 CE), and continued by her brother Ban Gu (32–92). Ban Zhao is credited with giving the Han Shu its present shape after the deaths of her father and brother, but she is most famous today for her advice book, directed toward young women.

I, the unworthy writer, am unsophisticated, unenlightened, and by nature unintelligent, but I am fortunate both to have received not a little favor from my scholarly Father, and to have had a cultured mother and instructresses upon whom to rely for a literary education as well as for training in good manners. More than forty years have passed since at the age of fourteen I took up the dustpan and the broom in the Cao family [the family into which she married]. During this time with trembling heart I feared constantly that I might disgrace my parents, and that I might multiply difficulties for both the women and the men of my husband's family. Day and night I was distressed in heart, but I labored without confessing weariness. Now and hereafter, however, I know how to escape from such fears.

Being careless, and by nature stupid, I taught and trained my children without system. Consequently I fear that my son Gu may bring disgrace upon the Imperial Dynasty by whose Holy Grace he has unprecedentedly received the extraordinary privilege of wearing the Gold and the Purple, a privilege for the attainment of which by my son, I a humble subject never even hoped. Nevertheless, now that he is a man and able to plan his own life, I need not again have concern for him. But I do grieve that you, my daughters, just now at the age for marriage, have not at this time had gradual training and advice; that you still have not learned the proper customs for married women. I fear that by failure in good manners in other families you will humiliate both your ancestors and your clan. I am now seriously ill, life is uncertain. As I have thought of you all in so untrained a state, I have been uneasy many a time for you. At hours of leisure I have composed . . . these instructions under the title, "Lessons for Women." In order

Source: Nancy Lee Swann, *Pan Chao: Foremost Woman Scholar of China* (New York: London Century, 1932), 82–90.

that you may have something wherewith to benefit your persons, I wish every one of you, my daughters each to write out a copy for yourself.

From this time on every one of you strive to practice these lessons.

HUMILITY

On the third day after the birth of a girl the ancients observed three customs: first to place the baby below the bed; second to give her a potsherd [a piece of broken pottery] with which to play; and third to announce her birth to her ancestors by an offering. Now to lay the baby below the bed plainly indicated that she is lowly and weak, and should regard it as her primary duty to humble herself before others. To give her potsherds with which to play indubitably signified that she should practice labor and consider it her primary duty to be industrious. To announce her birth before her ancestors clearly meant that she ought to esteem as her primary duty the continuation of the observance of worship in the home.

These three ancient customs epitomize woman's ordinary way of life and the teachings of the traditional ceremonial rites and regulations. Let a woman modestly yield to others; let her respect others; let her put others first, herself last. Should she do something good, let her not mention it; should she do something bad let her not deny it. Let her bear disgrace; let her even endure when others speak or do evil to her. Always let her seem to tremble and to fear. When a woman follows such maxims as these then she may be said to humble herself before others.

Let a woman retire late to bed, but rise early to duties; let her not dread tasks by day or by night. Let her not refuse to perform domestic duties whether easy or difficult. That which must be done, let her finish completely, tidily, and systematically. When a woman follows such rules as these, then she may be said to be industrious.

Let a woman be correct in manner and upright in character in order to serve her husband. Let her live in purity and quietness of spirit, and attend to her own affairs. Let her love not gossip and silly laughter. Let her cleanse and purify and arrange in order the wine and the food for the offerings to the ancestors. When a woman observes such principles as these, then she may be said to continue ancestral worship.

No woman who observes these three fundamentals of life has ever had a bad reputation or has fallen into disgrace. If a woman fail to observe them, how can her name be honored; how can she but bring disgrace upon herself?

. . .

IMPLICIT OBEDIENCE

Whenever the mother-in-law says, "Do not do that," and if what she says is right, unquestionably the daughter-in-law obeys. Whenever the mother-in-law says, "Do that," even if what she says is wrong, still the daughter-in-law submits unfailingly to the command. Let a woman not act contrary to the wishes and the opinions of parents-in-law about right and wrong; let her not dispute with them what is straight and what is crooked. Such docility may be called obedience which sacrifices personal opinion. Therefore the ancient book, "A Pattern for Women," says: "If a daughter-in-law who follows the wishes of her parents-in-law is like and echo and shadow, how could she not be praised?

WORKING WITH SOURCES

1. What does Ban Zhao tell us about the status of daughters-in-law in her culture? Are these fates capable to being avoided?
2. What should be the central and perennial activities of a woman's life, in the opinion of Ban Zhao? Did she conduct her own life differently?

10. ISLAMIC CIVILIZATION AND BYZANTIUM, 600–1300 CE

10.1 Excerpts from the Quran, *Sura* 2, "The Cow," ca. 650 CE

The name of the most holy book of Islam, the Quran, means "the recital." It contains, according to Islamic theology, the direct words of God (Allah), as told to his prophet Muhammad through the angel Gabriel. Muslims believe that the angel directed Muhammad to "recite" 114 *suras*, or books, beginning around 610 CE. After Muhammad's death in 632, an authorized text of these *suras* was compiled and publicized. The general arrangement of the Quran is according to the length of each document. It is important to note, therefore, that the Quran does not purport to be a continuous narrative, telling a series of stories, as is typical in other religious texts. This means that individual pronouncements can be taken out of context, and that various portions of the document can be quoted to different effects.

2:177
Righteousness is not that you turn your faces toward the east or the west, but [true] righteousness is [in] one who believes in Allah , the Last Day, the angels, the Book, and the prophets and gives wealth, in spite of love for it, to relatives, orphans, the needy, the traveler, those who ask [for help], and for freeing slaves; [and who] establishes prayer and gives *zakah* [charitable gifts]; [those who] fulfill their promise when they promise; and [those who] are patient in poverty and hardship and during battle. Those are the ones who have been true, and it is those who are the righteous.

2:178
O you who have believed, prescribed for you is legal retribution for those murdered—the free for the free, the slave for the slave, and the female for the female. But whoever overlooks from his brother anything, then there should be a suitable follow-up and payment to him with good conduct. This is an alleviation from your Lord and a mercy. But whoever transgresses after that will have a painful punishment.

2:179
And there is for you in legal retribution [saving of] life, O you [people] of understanding, that you may become righteous.

2:180
Prescribed for you when death approaches [any] one of you if he leaves wealth [is that he should make] a bequest for the parents and near relatives according to what is acceptable—a duty upon the righteous.

2:181
Then whoever alters the bequest after he has heard it—the sin is only upon those who have altered it. Indeed, Allah is Hearing and Knowing.

2:182
But if one fears from the bequeather [some] error or sin and corrects that which is between them, there

Source: Sahih International translation, available online at http://quran.com/4.

is no sin upon him. Indeed, Allah is Forgiving and Merciful.

2:183
O you who have believed, decreed upon you is fasting as it was decreed upon those before you that you may become righteous -

2:184
[Fasting for] a limited number of days. So whoever among you is ill or on a journey [during them]—then an equal number of days [are to be made up]. And upon those who are able [to fast, but with hardship]—a ransom [as substitute] of feeding a poor person [each day]. And whoever volunteers excess—it is better for him. But to fast is best for you, if you only knew.

2:185
The month of Ramadhan [is that] in which was revealed the Qur'an, a guidance for the people and clear proofs of guidance and criterion. So whoever sights [the new moon of] the month, let him fast it; and whoever is ill or on a journey—then an equal number of other days. Allah intends for you ease and does not intend for you hardship and [wants] for you to complete the period and to glorify Allah for that [to] which He has guided you; and perhaps you will be grateful.

2:186
And when My servants ask you, [O Muhammad], concerning Me—indeed I am near. I respond to the invocation of the supplicant when he calls upon Me. So let them respond to Me [by obedience] and believe in Me that they may be [rightly] guided.

2:187
It has been made permissible for you the night preceding fasting to go to your wives [for sexual relations]. They are clothing for you and you are clothing for them. Allah knows that you used to deceive yourselves, so He accepted your repentance and forgave you. So now, have relations with them and seek that which Allah has decreed for you. And eat and drink until the white thread of dawn becomes distinct to you from the black thread [of night]. Then complete the fast until the sunset. And do not have relations with them as long as you are staying for worship in the mosques. These are the limits [set by] Allah , so do not approach them. Thus does Allah make clear His ordinances to the people that they may become righteous.

2:188
And do not consume one another's wealth unjustly or send it [in bribery] to the rulers in order that [they might aid] you [to] consume a portion of the wealth of the people in sin, while you know [it is unlawful].

2:189
They ask you, [O Muhammad], about the new moons. Say, "They are measurements of time for the people and for Hajj." And it is not righteousness to enter houses from the back, but righteousness is [in] one who fears Allah. And enter houses from their doors. And fear Allah that you may succeed.

2:190
Fight in the way of Allah those who fight you but do not transgress. Indeed. Allah does not like transgressors.

2:191
And kill them wherever you overtake them and expel them from wherever they have expelled you, and fitnah [distress, civil strife, sedition] is worse than killing. And do not fight them at al-Masjid al- Haram until they fight you there. But if they fight you, then kill them. Such is the recompense of the disbelievers.

2:192
And if they cease, then indeed, Allah is Forgiving and Merciful.

2:193
Fight them until there is no [more] fitnah and [until] worship is [acknowledged to be] for Allah . But if they cease, then there is to be no aggression except against the oppressors.

2:194
[Fighting in] the sacred month is for [aggression committed in] the sacred month, and for [all] violations is legal retribution. So whoever has assaulted you, then assault him in the same way that he has assaulted you. And fear Allah and know that Allah is with those who fear Him.

2:195
And spend in the way of Allah and do not throw [yourselves] with your [own] hands into destruction [by refraining]. And do good; indeed, Allah loves the doers of good.

WORKING WITH SOURCES

1. What are the requirements of believers, and what benefits and punishments are promised in response to their actions?
2. Why is it important to observe the rules regarding fasting and the pilgrimage?

10.2 Documents Related to the Iconoclasm Controversy, Seventh–Ninth Centuries CE

The Byzantine Empire was racked by a series of religious disputes that pulled in emperors as well as priests. One of the most significant of these was an ongoing difference of opinion concerning "graven images" of Jesus and other prominent figures in Christian narratives. Was it proper to create and display images of God, and, if so, should existing "icons" be destroyed in order to protect the faithful? These documents represent the two major perspectives on this debate, between the poles of the "iconodule" (pro-icon) position and the "iconoclastic" (anti-icon) position.

ICONODULE POSITION:

1 Quinsextum Council (in Trullo), 692 CE, ruling by Justinian II (685–695; 705–711):

"Now, in order that perfection be represented before the eyes of all people, even in paintings, we ordain that from now on Christ our God, the Lamb who took upon Himself the sins of the world, be set up, even in images according to His human character, instead of the ancient Lamb. Through this figure we realize the height of the humiliation of God the Word and are led to remember His life in the flesh, His suffering, and His saving death, and the redemption ensuing from it for the world."

2 John of Damascus (675–749), Oration (PG 94, cols. 1258C-D):

"When we set up an image of Christ in any place, we appeal to the senses, and indeed we sanctify the sense of sight, which is the highest among the perceptive senses, just as by sacred speech we sanctify the sense of hearing. An image is, after all, a reminder; it is to the illiterate what a book is to the literate, and what the word is to the hearing, the image is to sight. We remember that God ordered that a vessel be made from wood that would not rot, gilded inside and out, and that the tables of the law should be placed in it and the staff and the golden vessel containing the manna—all this for a reminder of what had taken place, and a foreshadowing of what was to come. What was this but a visual image, more compelling than any sermon? And this sacred thing was not placed in some obscure corner of the tabernacle; it was displayed in full view of the people, so that whenever they looked at it they would give honor and worship to the God Who had through its contents made known His design to them. They were of course not worshipping the things themselves; they were being led through them to recall the wonderful works of God, and to adore Him Whose words they had witnessed."

Source: excerpts from Anthony Bryer and Judith Herrin, eds., *Iconoclasm: Papers Given at the Ninth Spring Symposium of Byzantine Studies, University of Birmingham, March 1975* (Birmingham, UK: Centre for Byzantine Studies, University of Birmingham, 1977), available online at http://www.tulane.edu/~august/H303/readings/Iconoclasm.htm.

3 Horos (Definition of Faith) at the Seventh Ecumenical Council, Nicaea, 787 CE:

"We define with accuracy and care that the venerable and holy icons be set up like the form of the venerable and life-giving Cross, inasmuch as the matter consisting of colors and pebbles and other matter is appropriate in the holy church of God, on sacred vessels and vestments, walls and panels, in houses and on the roads, as well as the images of our Lord and God and Savior Jesus Christ, of our undefiled Lady of the Holy Mother of God, of the angels worthy of honor, and of all the holy and pious men. For the more frequently they are seen by means of pictorial representation the more those who behold them are aroused to remember and desire the prototypes and to give them greeting and worship of honor—but not the true worship of our faith which befits only the divine nature—but to offer them both incense and candles, in the same way as to the form and the venerable and life-giving Cross and the holy Gospel and to the other sacred objects, as was the custom even of the ancients."

ICONOCLASTIC POSITION:

1 The Horos (Definition of Faith) at the Council of Hiera, 754 CE:

"The divine nature is completely uncircumscribable and cannot be depicted or represented in any medium whatsoever. The word Christ means both God and Man, and an icon of Christ would therefore have to be an image of God in the flesh of the Son of God. But this is impossible. The artist would fall either into the heresy which claims that the divine and human natures of Christ are separate or into that which holds that there is only one nature of Christ."

2 The Horos (Definition of Faith) at Iconoclastic Council of 815 CE:

"Wherefore, taking to heart the correct doctrine, we banish from the Catholic Church the unwarranted manufacture of the spurious icons that has been so audaciously proclaimed, impelled as we are by a judicious judgment; nay, by passing a righteous judgment upon the veneration of icons that has been injudiciously proclaimed by Tarasius [Patriarch, 784–802] and so refuting it, we declare his assembly [i.e. Seventh Ecumenical Council in 787] invalid in that it bestowed exaggerated honor to painting, namely, as has already been said, the lighting of candles and lamps and the offering of incense, these marks of veneration being those of worship. We gladly accept, on the other hand, the pious council that was held at Blachernae, in the church of the all-pure Virgin, under the pious Emperors Constantine V and Leo IV [in 754] that was fortified by the doctrine of the Fathers, and in preserving without alteration what was expressed by it, we decree that the manufacture of icons is unfit for veneration and useless. We refrain, however, from calling them idols since there is a distinction between different kinds of evil."

WORKING WITH SOURCES

1. Do you find one of the positions in this theological debate more convincing than the other? Why?
2. Was it necessary for the Byzantine emperors to intervene in this controversy? Why or why not?

10.3 Memoirs of Usama Ibn Munqidh, ca. 1180s

A scholar, a gentleman, and a warrior, Usama (1095–1187) had ample opportunity to meet Crusader forces in person on the battlefield and in civilian life. After a distinguished military career, he became a consultant and advisor to Saladin in 1174, and he oversaw the surrender of Beirut, as its governor, to Crusader forces. Basking in Saladin's favor, Usama became the center of attention in Damascus. He began a memoir describing the various peoples whom he had encountered during his long and adventurous life. His observations are often humorous, sometimes baffling, but always imbued with curiosity about people whose customs are strange—and intriguing.

Among the Frankish [i.e., Crusaders, known to Arabs as "al-Franjj"] captives who were carried into my father's home was an aged woman accompanied by her daughter—a young woman of great beauty—and a robust son. The son accepted Islam, and his conversion was genuine, judging by what he showed in the practice of prayer and fasting. He learned the art of working marble from a stonecutter who had paved the home of my father. After staying for a long time with us my father gave him as wife a woman who belonged to a pious family, and paid all necessary expenses for his wedding and home. His wife bore him two sons. The boys grew up. When they were five or six years old, their father, young Rā'ūl, who was very happy at having them, took them with their mother and everything that his house contained and on the second morning joined the Franks in Afāmiyah, where he and his children became Christians after having practiced Islam with its prayers and faith. May Allah, therefore, purify the world from such people!

Mysterious are the works of the Creator, the author of all things! When one comes to recount cases regarding the Franks, he cannot but glorify Allah (exalted is he!) and sanctify him, for he sees them as animals possessing the virtues of courage and fighting, but nothing else; just as animals have only the virtues of strength and carrying loads. I shall now give some instances of their doings and their curious mentality.

. . .

The king of the Franks [Fulk of Anjou, king of Jerusalem] had for treasurer a knight named Bernard, who (may Allah's curse be upon him!) was one of the most accursed and wicked among the Franks. A horse kicked him in the leg, which was subsequently infected and which opened in fourteen different places. Every time one of these cuts would close in one place, another would open in another place. All this happened while I was praying for his perdition. Then came to him a Frankish physician and removed from the leg all the ointments which were on it and began to wash it with very strong vinegar. By this treatment all the cuts were healed and the man became well again. He was up again like a devil.

Another case illustrating their curious medicine is the following:

In Shayzar we had an artisan named abu-al-Fath, who had a boy whose neck was afflicted with scrofula. Every time a part of it would close, another part would open. This man happened to go to Antioch on business of his, accompanied by his son. A Frank

Source: An Arab-Syrian Gentleman and Warrior in the Period of the Crusades: Memoirs of Usāmah ibn-Munqidh, trans. Philip K. Hitti (Princeton, NJ: Princeton University Press, 1987), 160–161, 162–163, and 164–165.

noticed the boy and asked his father about him, "Wilt thou swear by thy religion that if I prescribe to thee a medicine which will cure thy boy, thou wilt charge nobody fees for prescribing it thyself? In that case, I shall prescribe to thee a medicine which will cure the boy." The man took the oath and the Frank said:

"Take uncrushed leaves of glasswort, burn them, then soak the ashes in olive oil and sharp vinegar. Treat the scrofula with them until the spot on which it is growing is eaten up. Then take burnt lead, soak it in ghee butter and treat him with it. That will cure him."

The father treated the boy accordingly, and the boy was cured. The sores closed and the boy returned to his normal condition of health.

I have myself treated with this medicine many who were afflicted with such disease, and the treatment was successful in removing the cause of the complaint.

. . .

Here is an illustration which I myself witnessed:

When I used to visit Nāblus, I always took lodging with a man named Mu'izz, whose home was a lodging house for the Moslems. The house had windows which opened to the road, and there stood opposite to it on the other side of the road a house belonging to a Frank who sold wine for the merchants. He would take some wine in a bottle and go around announcing it by shouting, "So and so, the merchant, has just opened a cask full of this wine. He who wants to buy some of it will find it in such and such a place." The Frank's pay for the announcement made would be the wine in that bottle. One day this Frank went home and found a man with his wife in the same bed. He asked him, "What could have made thee enter into my wife's room?" The man replied, "I was tired, so I went in to rest." "But how," asked he, "didst thou get into my bed?" The other replied, "I found a bed that was spread, so I slept in it." "But," said he, "my wife was sleeping together with thee!" The other replied, "Well, the bed is hers. How could I therefore have prevented her from using her own bed?" "By the truth of my religion," said the husband, "if thou shouldst do it again, thou and I would have a quarrel." Such was for the Frank the entire expression of his disapproval and the limit of his jealousy.

WORKING WITH SOURCES

1. What proof does Usama offer of the uncivilized nature of the Christian invaders of the Middle East?
2. How does he demonstrate Islamic cultural, if not always military, superiority in his account?

10.4 A Jewish Engagement Contract from Fustat (Old Cairo), 11 November 1146

A treasure trove of letters, contracts, legal instruments, etc., known as the Cairo Geniza, attests to the lives of both prominent and average Jewish people, especially in the eleventh and twelfth centuries. Due to their *dhimma* status (that is, officially recognized religious minorities in a predominantly Muslim state), Jews lived under the constant threat of reprisals and violent raids throughout the Middle East (as well as in Europe) in this period. Nevertheless, they were also able to engage in normal business and personal activities, and these documents provide a welcome window into daily life.

Source: S. D. Goitein, *A Mediterranean Society: The Jewish Communities of the Arab World as Portrayed in the Documents of the Cairo Geniza*, vol. 4 (Berkeley: University of California Press, 1983), 317–319.

This is a copy of the engagement contract of Abū Mansūr Semah, son of Rabbānā Japheth [known as] the elder Abū Alī, the perfumer, to Sitt al-Khāssa, the daughter of the elder Abu 'l-Barakāt Ibn al-Lebdī.

On Monday, the fifth day of the month of Kislev of the year 1458 of the era of the documents, in Fustat, Egypt, which is situated on the Nile River and which is under the jurisdiction of our lord Samuel, the great Nagrid—may his name be forever, M. Semah, the young man, son of M. and R. Japheth the elder, son of M. and R. Tiqvā, the elder, the Friend of the yeshiva—may he rest in Eden—concluded a match with Sitt al-Khāssa, his fiancée, a virgin, the daughter of M. and R. Berakhōt, the elder—may he rest in Eden.

His obligation is a first installment of 40 certified dinars, to be given as a gift at the time of the wedding, and a final installment of 100 certified dinars. Abū Mansūr Semah, the fiancé, presented the 40 dinars of the first installment, and the elder Abu 'l-Alā' Musallam, the perfumer, son of Sahl, received them from him. The wedding is set for the month of Kislev of the coming year—may we be destined for life in it—which is the coming year 1459 [1147].

Semah assumed these obligations toward Sitt al-Khāssa: She will be regarded as trustworthy in all that concerns food and drink in the house, no suspicion may be cast upon her, nor can he demand from her an oath concerning any of these things, not even a supplementary oath. He may not marry another woman, nor retain a maidservant whom she dislikes. Should he do any of these things, the final installment is hers, and he must release her [from the marriage bond by divorce]. In the case that there are no children, half of what remains of the dowry returns to her family. She may choose the place and the domicile where she wishes to live. The rent of her properties is hers, she may spend it for whatever purpose she prefers; he has no say in the matter.

Should he nullify this engagement contract and not marry her during the said Kislev, she will receive 20 dinars. This is a debt and an obligation, binding [as from now]. We made the symbolic purchase from M. Semah, the young man, for Sitt al-Khāssa, the fiancée, according to all that is recorded above, a purchase which is definite and strict, made with the proper object for such a transaction.

We also made the symbolic purchase from Sitt al-Sāda, the daughter of the elder Abū Nasr, the physician, the mother of Sitt al-Khāssa, the fiancée, in the most rigorous terms, binding as from now: Should her daughter Sitt al-Khāssa nullify the engagement contract and refuse to marry the fiancé during the said month of Kislev, she would owe the fiancé 20 [dinars]. . . . This has taken place after the verification of her identity.

Signatures: Mevōrākh b. Solomon [of] b[lessed] m[emory]. Sadaqa b__________.

WORKING WITH SOURCES

1. Are the parties to this contract anxious to demonstrate, particularly to Muslim officials, that they understand business affairs and can conduct them sensibly among themselves?
2. What differences are reflected in this document between the roles of women and men with respect to marriage?

10.5 *The Alchemy of Happiness*, by Abd al-Hamid al-Ghazali, ca. 1095–1105

Born in 1058 to a family of spinners and sellers of wool in a small village in eastern Iran, Ghazali became one of the most prominent expounders of Islamic theology of his day. Traveling

Source: Abū Hāmid Muhammad al-Ghazzālī, *The Alchemy of Happiness*, trans. Claud Field (Armonk, NY: M. E. Sharpe, 1991), 6–7 and 11–13.

widely, from Persia to Baghdad to Damascus, he mastered a wide range of disciplines, and he energetically engaged in arguments with those he considered extremists. When he died in 1111, he left behind a series of treatises, many of them incorporating autobiographical material, particularly the discoveries he had himself made and was fully capable of defending.

The first step to self-knowledge is to know that thou art composed of an outward shape, called the body, and an inward entity called the heart or soul. By "heart" I do not mean the piece of flesh situated in the left of our bodies, but that which uses all the other faculties as its instruments and servants. In truth it does not belong to the visible world, but to the invisible, and has come into this world as a traveler visits a foreign country for the sake of merchandise, and it will presently return to its native land. It is the knowledge of this entity and its attributes which is the key to the knowledge of God.

. . .

A mistake of an opposite kind is made by shallow people who, echoing some phrases which they have caught from Sufi teachers, go about decrying all knowledge. This is as if a person who was not an adept in alchemy were to go about saying, "Alchemy is better than gold," and were to refuse gold when it was offered to him. Alchemy is better than gold, but real alchemists are very rare, and so are real Sufis. He who has a mere smattering of Sufism is not superior to a learned man, any more than he who has tried a few experiments in alchemy has ground for despising a rich man.

Anyone who will look into the matter will see that happiness is necessarily linked with the knowledge of God. Each faculty of ours delights in that for which it was created: lust delights in accomplishing desire, anger in taking vengeance, the eye in seeing beautiful objects, and the ear in hearing harmonious sounds. The highest function of the soul of man is the perception of truth; in this accordingly it finds its special delight. Even in trifling matters, such as learning chess, this holds good, and the higher the subject-matter of the knowledge obtained, the greater the delight. A man would be pleased at being admitted into the confidence of a prime minister, but how much more if the king makes an intimate of him and discloses state secrets to him!

An astronomer who, by his knowledge, can map the stars and describe their courses, derives more pleasure from his knowledge than the chess-player from his. Seeing, then, that nothing is higher than God, how great must be the delight which springs from the true knowledge of Him!

. . .

Man has been truly termed a "microcosm", or little world in himself, and the structures of his body should be studied not only by those who wish to become doctors, but by those who wish to attain to a more intimate knowledge of God, just as close study of the niceties and shades of language in a great poem reveals to us more and more of the genius of its author.

WORKING WITH SOURCES

1. How does Ghazali demonstrate an understanding of "science," and which specific sciences does he reference?
2. Why is he angry at the Sufis? Is his analysis of the problems posed by some Sufis justified?

11. INNOVATION AND ADAPTATION IN THE WESTERN CHRISTIAN WORLD, 600–1450 CE

11.1 Einhard's *Life of Charlemagne*, ca. 830 CE

The model for Einhard's *Vita Caroli Magni* was Suetonius's biographies of the first twelve Roman emperors, and particularly of Augustus, composed in the second century CE. The biography is thus an example of the general attempt to revive interest in and appreciation for pre-Christian Roman antiquity in the midst of the "Carolingian Renaissance," of which Einhard was both a product and a driving force. Educated at the Palace School at Aachen (Charlemagne's capital), Einhard established a close personal and professional connection with the man himself. Due to his intimate knowledge of Charlemagne's behavior, habits, and outlook, Einhard was ideally placed to write his biography, which was composed after Charlemagne's death but contained pointed advice to the man's successors.

§24: . . . His main meal of the day was served in four courses, in addition to the roast meat which his hunters used to bring in on spits and which he enjoyed more than any other food. During his meal he would listen to a public reading or some other entertainment. Stories would be recited for him, or the doings of the ancients told again. He took great pleasure in the books of Saint Augustine and especially in those which are called *The City of God*.

. . .

§25 He spoke easily and fluently, and could express with great clarity whatever he had to say. He was not content with his own mother tongue, but took the trouble to learn foreign languages. He learnt Latin so well that he spoke it as fluently as his own tongue; but he understood Greek better than he could speak it. He was eloquent to the point of sometimes seeming almost garrulous.

He paid the greatest attention to the liberal arts; and he had great respect for men who taught them, bestowing high honours upon them. When he was learning the rules of grammar he received tuition from Peter the Deacon of Pisa, who by then was an old man, but for all other subjects he was taught by Alcuin, surnamed Albinus, another Deacon, a man of the Saxon race who came from Britain and was the most learned man anywhere to be found. Under him the Emperor spent much time and effort in studying rhetoric, dialectic and especially astrology. He applied himself to mathematics and traced the course of the stars with great attention and care. He also tried to learn to write. With this object in view he used to keep writing-tablets and notebooks under the pillows on his bed, so that he could try his hand at forming letters during his leisure moments; but, although he tried very hard, he had begun too late in life and he made little progress.

§26 Charlemagne practised the Christian religion with great devotion and piety, for he had been brought up in this faith since earliest childhood. . . . He donated

---

Source: TWO LIVES OF CHARLEMAGNE by Einhard and Notker the Stammerer, translated with an introduction by Professor Lewis Thorpe (Penguin Classics, 1969), 78–80.

so many sacred vessels made of gold and silver, and so many priestly vestments, that when service time came even those who opened and closed the doors, surely the humblest of all church dignitaries, had no need to perform their duties in their everyday clothes. He made careful reforms in the way in which the psalms were chanted and the lessons read. He was himself quite an expert at both of these exercises, but he never read the lesson in public and he would sing only with the rest of the congregation and then in a low voice.

WORKING WITH SOURCES

1. How does this passage reflect the attempt to recreate the ancient past during the Carolingian Renaissance?
2. Did Charlemagne separate his private life from his public image? Why?

11.2 Feudal Contracts and the Swearing of Fealty, 1127 and 1219

In the catastrophe brought on by the assaults on all their borders, some European Christians were forced to devise new means of self-protection. Into this vacuum of governmental authority came new "feudal" relationships between lords and vassals. Over time, these contractual relationships became increasingly regularized. The terms of these relationships can be reconstructed through documents describing the ceremonial and formulaic aspects of feudal obligations.

How the Count of Flanders received the homage of his vassals (1127):

Through the whole remaining part of the day those who had been previously **enfeoffed** by the most pious Count Charles did homage to the [new] count, taking up now again their fiefs and offices and whatever they had before rightfully and legitimately obtained. On Thursday, the seventh of April, homages were again made to the count, being completed in the following order of faith and security.

First they did their homage thus. The count asked the vassal if he were willing to become completely his man, and the other replied, "I am willing"; and with hands clasped, placed between the hands of the count, they were bound together by a kiss. Secondly, he who had done homage gave his fealty to the representative of the count in these words, "I promise on my faith that I will in future be faithful to Count William, and will observe my homage to him completely against all persons, in good faith and without deceit." And, thirdly, he took his oath to this upon the relics of the saints. Afterward the count, with a little rod which he held in his hand, gave investitures to all who by this agreement had given their security and accompanying oath.

Pons of Mont-Saint-Jean becomes the man of the Countess of Champagne (1219):

I, Pons of Mont-Saint-Jean, make known to all, both present and future, that since I have long been the man

Enfeoffed: Invested with an estate, or "fief".

Source: James Harvey Robinson, *Readings in European History*, vol. 1 (Boston: Ginn & Company, 1904), 178–180.

of my beloved Lady Blanche, countess of Champagne, for twenty pounds assigned to the fair at Bar, and since later both the countess and my dear lord have added other twenty pounds assigned to the same fair and gave me three hundred pounds in cash,—I swore by the saints that I would in good faith aid them and their heirs with my people and fortifications. If necessary I will fight especially against Erard of Brienne and Philippa his wife, and against Adelaide, queen of Cyprus, and her heirs, and against all who would aid them; except that should the said countess or count or their people be against Milo of Noyers, my sister's husband, in his castle of Noyers or elsewhere in his lands, neither I nor my people shall be held to go thither. If, however, the said Milo or his people set upon the countess or the count or their people, we shall be held to defend them and their lands with all our might.

It is also to be known that my heir who shall hold Charniacum shall also have the fief above mentioned of forty pounds.

That all this shall be held valid, I corroborate what has here been written with the impression of my seal. Done in the year of grace 1219, in the month of June.

WORKING WITH SOURCES

1. Why are religious terms invoked so often in these documents in order to solidify the relationships between lords and vassals?
2. Did feudal contracts with women differ from those with men?

11.3 Peter Abelard, *The Story of My Misfortunes*, ca. 1132

One of the most brilliant professors and theologians of the European Middle Ages, Peter Abelard (1070–1142) became a star performer in the academic art of "dialectic." His abilities also earned him many enemies. When he turned his attention to the thorny subject of the Trinity, one of the principal elements of Christian belief, Abelard incurred the wrath of powerful members of the institutional church, of which he, as a professor, was also a part. In his autobiography, *The Story of My Misfortunes*, Abelard detailed the episodes of envy, backbiting, and stupidity that dogged him throughout his life. He also recalled his affair with Heloise (d. 1163), his former pupil and intellectual equal. The letters they exchanged survive as some of the most passionate and beautiful documents of the period.

It so happened that at the outset I devoted myself to analysing the basis of our faith through illustrations based on human understanding, and I wrote for my students a certain tract on the unity and trinity of God. This I did because they were always seeking for rational and philosophical explanations, asking rather for reasons they could understand than for mere words, saying that it was futile to utter words which the intellect could not possibly follow, that nothing could be believed unless it could first be understood, and that it was absurd for any one to preach to others a thing which neither he himself

Source: *The Story of My Misfortunes: The Autobiography of Peter Abélard*, trans. Henry Adams Bellows (New York: Macmillan, 1922), 36–44.

nor those whom he sought to teach could comprehend. Our Lord Himself maintained this same thing when He said: "They are blind leaders of the blind" (Matthew, xv, 14).

Now, a great many people saw and read this tract, and it became exceedingly popular, its clearness appealing particularly to all who sought information on this subject. And since the questions involved are generally considered the most difficult of all, their complexity is taken as the measure of the subtlety of him who succeeds in answering them. As a result, my rivals became furiously angry, and summoned a council to take action against me, the chief instigators therein being my two intriguing enemies of former days, Alberic and Lotulphe.

. . .

On one occasion Alberic, accompanied by some of his students, came to me for the purpose of intimidating me, and, after a few bland words, said that he was amazed at something he had found in my book, to the effect that, although God had begotten God, I denied that God had begotten Himself, since there was only one God. I answered unhesitatingly: "I can give you an explanation of this if you wish it." "Nay," he replied, "I care nothing for human explanation or reasoning in such matters, but only for the words of authority." "Very well," I said; "turn the pages of my book and you will find the authority likewise." The book was at hand, for he had brought it with him. I turned to the passage I had in mind, which he had either not discovered or else passed over as containing nothing injurious to me. And it was God's will that I quickly found what I sought. This was the following sentence, under the heading "Augustine, On the Trinity, Book I": "Whosoever believes that it is within the power of God to beget Himself is sorely in error; this power is not in God, neither is it in any created thing, spiritual or corporeal. For there is nothing that can give birth to itself."

When those of his followers who were present heard this, they were amazed and much embarrassed.

. . .

Straightway upon my summons I went to the council, and there, without further examination or debate, did they compel me with my own hand to cast that memorable book of mine into the flames.

WORKING WITH SOURCES

1. Explain the positions of Abelard and Alberic concerning "logic" and "faith" in this regard.
2. How does Abelard turn the tables on Alberic in his line of reasoning?

11.4 Giovanni Boccaccio, *The Decameron*, "Putting the Devil Back in Hell," ca. 1350

A Latin scholar, poet, and biographer, Boccaccio (1313–1375) is most famous today as the author of the *Decameron*. This compilation of 100 tales, by turns serious, bawdy, and irreverent, purports to be a rendition of the stories told over the course of 10 days by 10 young men and women who had fled Florence to escape the Black Death. Many of the tales are based on older legends, and they frequently reflect the humor of the common people of the era, often at the expense of their spiritual and social betters. Religious authorities were frequent targets of this sort of satire, reflecting their ubiquitous presence in the lives of medieval Europeans, as well as, perhaps, a deep undercurrent of resentment regarding their privileges.

Source: Giovanni Boccaccio, "Putting the Devil Back in Hell" (3.10), from *The Decameron: Selected Tales / Decameron: Novelle scelte*, trans. Stanley Appelbaum (Mineola, NY: Dover, 2000), 87–93.

. . . And so, coming to the facts, I say that in the city of Gafsa in Tunisia there was once a very rich man who, among other children, had a beautiful and genteel daughter named Alibec. She, not being a Christian, but hearing many Christians who lived in the city praising the Christian religion and the service of God, asked one of them one day how God could be served in the easiest way. This man replied that God was best served by those who fled worldly things, like those men who had gone into the lonely deserts of the Thebaid.

[Alibec goes into the desert, seeking out a willing hermit, and finally arrives at the door of a man who is willing to help her.]

. . . She reached the cell of a young hermit, a very devout and kind person named Rustico, and asked him the same thing she had asked the others.

. . .

First feeling his way with certain questions, he learned that she had never slept with a man and was just as naïve as she looked. And so he planned a way to have her submit to his pleasure under the pretext of serving God. First he told her at length that the devil was the enemy of God; then he gave her to understand that the service most pleasing to God was putting the devil back in hell, to which place God had condemned him.

The girl asked him how that was done, and Rustico replied: "You'll soon know; to make it happen, do what you see me doing." And he began to take off the few garments he was wearing until he was stark naked; and the girl did the same. Then he knelt down as if he were going to pray, and he made her do the same, facing him.

As they knelt there, Rustico's desire flared up more than ever at the sight of her great beauty, and there ensued the resurrection of the flesh. Seeing that and wondering at it, Alibec said: "Rustico, what's that thing I see on you sticking out like that? I don't have one."

"My daughter," said Rustico, "that's the devil I told you about. And now look: he's giving me terrible discomfort, so that I can hardly stand it."

Then the girl said: "Praised be God, for I see that I'm better off than you, because I don't have that devil!"

Rustico said: "It's true, but you have something else that I don't have, and you have it in place of this."

Alibec said: "What is it?"

Rustico replied: "You have hell, and, believe me, I think God has sent you here to save my soul, because, whenever this devil causes me this distress, if you want to take pity on me and let me put him back in hell, you will give me the greatest relief, and you're doing God the greatest pleasure and service—if you've really come to this area for that purpose, as you say."

The girl replied in good faith: "Oh, Father, since I have hell, let it be whenever you like."

Then Rustico said: "Bless you, daughter! Let's go put him back so he'll leave me in peace."

Saying that, he led the girl to one of their pallets and taught her how to position herself to imprison that being who was accursed of God.

. . .

[After a fire destroys much of Gafsa, Alibec is the only surviving heir to her father's property, and she is married to a young man named Neerbal.]

But, being asked by the ladies what she had done to serve God in the desert—this was before Neerbal had slept with her—she replied that she had served Him by putting the devil back in hell, and that Neerbal had committed a great sin by taking her away from that service. The ladies asked: "How is the devil put back in hell?"

Partly with words and partly with gestures, the girl showed them how. They laughed so loud at this that they're still laughing, and they said: "Don't fret, youngster, no, because that's done here, too; Neerbal and you will do God good service that way."

WORKING WITH SOURCES

1. Is Alibec's naïveté designed to convey a warning to the reader?
2. Does this tale reflect a mocking attitude toward *all* forms of religiosity?

11.5 Flagellants Attempt to Ward Off the Black Death in Germany and in England, 1348 and 1349

Although flagellation (beating oneself with a whip) had been practiced as a means of spiritual discipline by monks long before, it did not emerge as a public group activity until the thirteenth century. While Europe was besieged by the Black Death (1348–1352), the Brotherhood of Flagellants (which also included women) resorted to ever more spectacular public flagellation. The movement probably originated in eastern Europe and took root most deeply in German-speaking areas, as the account below demonstrates. As we see from the subsequent report of Robert of Avesbury, however, they had also crossed into England, offering some sort of solution to the plague crisis.

In 1348 a race without a head aroused universal wonder by their sudden appearance in huge numbers. They suddenly sprang up in all parts of Germany, calling themselves cross bearers or flagellants.

. . .

They were called flagellants because of the whips [*flagella*] which they used in performing public penance. Each whip consisted of a stick with three knotted thongs hanging from the end. Two pieces of needle-sharp metal were run through the centre of the knots from both sides, forming a cross, the ends of which extended beyond the knots for the length of a grain of wheat or less. Using these whips they beat and whipped their bare skin until their bodies were bruised and swollen and blood rained down, spattering the walls nearby. I have seen, when they whipped themselves, how sometimes those bits of metal penetrated the flesh so deeply that it took more than two attempts to pull them out.

Flocking together from every region, perhaps even from every city, they overran the whole land. In open country they straggled along behind the cross in no particular order, but when they came to cities, towns and villages they formed themselves into a procession, with hoods or hats pulled down over their foreheads, and sad and downcast eyes, they went through the streets singing a sweet hymn. In this fashion they entered the church and shut themselves in while they stripped off their clothes and left them with a guard.

. . .

After this, one of them would strike the first with a whip, saying, "May God grant you remission of all your sins. Arise." And he would get up, and do the same to the second, and all the others in turn did the same. When they were all on their feet, and arranged two by two in procession, two of them in the middle of the column would begin singing a hymn in a high voice, with a sweet melody.

[From Robert of Avesbury:]
In that same year of 1349, about Michaelmas [29 September], more than 120 men, for the most part from Zeeland or Holland, arrived in London from Flanders. These went barefoot in procession twice a day in the sight of the people, sometimes in St Paul's church and sometimes elsewhere in the city, their bodies naked except for a linen cloth from loins to ankle. Each wore a hood painted with a red cross at front and back and carried in his right hand a whip with three thongs. Each thong had a knot in it, with something sharp, like a needle, stuck through the middle of the knot so that it stuck out on each side, and as they walked one after the other they struck

Source: "52. The Flagellants," from the *Chronicon Henrici de Hervordia and from the Concerning the Miraculous Deeds of King Edward III* by Robert of Avesbury, in Rosemary Horrox, *The Black Death* (Manchester, UK: Manchester University Press, 1994), 150–154.

themselves with these whips on their naked, bloody bodies; four of them singing in their own tongue and the rest answering in the manner of the Christian litany. Three times in each procession they would all prostrate themselves on the ground, with their arms outstretched in the shape of a cross. Still singing, and beginning with the man at the end, each in turn would step over the others, lashing the man beneath him once with his whip, until all of those lying down had gone through the same ritual. Then each one put on his usual clothes and, always with their hoods on their heads and carrying their whips, they departed to their lodgings. It was said that they performed a similar penance every night.

WORKING WITH SOURCES

1. What did the Flagellants think was the source and cause of the plague?
2. How might their behavior have made matters worse for the observers?

12. CONTRASTING PATTERNS IN INDIA AND CHINA, 600–1600 CE

12.1 *The Chachnamah*, ca. 1200

Composed in Arabic and translated into Persian in the twelfth and thirteenth centuries, the *Chachnamah* details the Arab conquest of the Sind (a province corresponding to northwest India and Pakistan) in the eighth century. The work details the campaign by Muhammad Ibn Qasim, which was the most successful of the many attempts by Muslims to conquer the region. In this history of the campaign, Ibn Qasim is both a conquering hero and a defender of Islam, subduing non-Muslims and imposing new religious values in his wake.

A description of the battle.
Hazlí states that, in that army of the Arabs there was a brave soldier by name Háris son of Marrah. He was at the head of a column of one thousand fully armed warriors. He had three brave slaves with him, one of whom he retained to bear his arms, and the other two he appointed as officers in the army, each being made the leader of 500 men. When they arrived at Makrán the news was carried to Kíkánán, where the people prepared for battle and commenced fighting. They were about 20,000 men. (Nevertheless) the army of Islám attacked them and overpowered them, and seeing no other help, the natives retreated to the gates of the town. But when the Arab army left the battlefield and marched after the residents of Kíkánán, the latter came down to obstruct their progress. The Arab army made an onset, with their war cry of "Alláhu Akbar" (God is great) and from the left and the right the cliffs echoed the cry of "Alláhu Akbar." When the infidels of Kíkánán heard those cries they were much frightened, and some of them surrendered and accepted Islám and the rest fled away, and from that time up to our day, on the anniversary of that battle, cries of "Alláhu Akbar" are heard from the mountain.

They had already completed this victory when they received the sad news of the martyrdom of His Highness the Commander of the Faithful, Alí son of Abí Tálib, (on whom be peace). They, therefore, turned back, and when they arrived at Makrán, they learnt that Muáwiyeh son of Abísafiyán had become the Khalífah.

. . .

A tradition.
It is related by Abul Hasan, who heard it from Hazlí, and Hazlí from Muslim son of Muhárib son of Muslim son of Ziyád, that when Muáwiyeh despatched the expedition of 4,000 men under Abdulláh son of Sawád, no one had to kindle fire in his camp, as they had carried abundant provisions for the journey, ready made for use. It was only on a single night that fire-light was perceived in the camp, and, on enquiry being made, it was found that a pregnant woman had been confined and fire was urgently required. Abdulláh gave her permission and she gave a merry banquet, and for three days continually entertained the whole army (with fresh-cooked food).

Source: The Chachnamah: An Ancient History of Sind, trans. Mirza Kalichbeg Fredunbeg, available online at http://persian.packhum.org/persian/main?url=pf%3Ffile%3D12701030%26ct%3D0.

When Abdulláh arrived at Kíkánán, the enemy made an assault on him, but the army of Islám routed them, and secured plenty of booty. The people of Kíkánán assembled in large numbers, and occupied the mountain passes. The battle now raged furiously and Abdulláh son of Sawád found it necessary to keep his men in their ranks, by making a stand himself with a party of selected men, fully armed; and he appealed to the hearts of others in the following words: "O children of the Prophet's companions, do not turn your faces from the infidels, so that your faith may remain free from any flaw and you acquire the honour of martyrdom." Hearing these words his men assembled round the standard of Abdulláh, and one of these men, who belonged to the family of Abdul Kais, came out with a challenge to a single fight. Instantly the chief of the enemy's forces engaged with him. The example of this hero was followed by another Yásar son of Sawád. The chief was killed, but the army of Kíkánán made a general assault, by which the army of Islám was ultimately put to flight. The whole mountainous region now became alive with fighting men and the Musalmans beat a (hasty) retreat, and came back to Makrán.

A tradition.

Abul Hasan relates that he heard Hátim son of Kutai-bíah Sahlí say: "That day I myself was in the army when the son of Sawád fought with his youthful adversary, and his friends advanced in the same manner, and killed many men of the enemy's side. After a hard fight they at last fell martyrs and I stripped the dead bodies of the enemy, and found a hundred signet rings."

. . .

Safyán son of U'r dí appointed to carry on the religious war in Hind.

It is related by Hazlí who heard it from Tibuí son of Músá, who again heard it from his father, that on Abdulláh son of Sawád being martyred, he appointed Sinán son of Salmah as his successor. Soon afterwards Muáwiyeh wrote to Ziyád, (the then governor of Irák) to select a proper person for the holy wars in Hind. When he received the letter, Ziyád nominated Ahnaf son of Kais, who was liked by all, and was the pride of the Faithful. Ahnaf forthwith went to Makrán, where he remained for a period of two years, and after two years and one month he was removed from that post.

WORKING WITH SOURCES

1. To what extent is this conflict envisioned as a "religious war"?
2. Why does the document concern itself with successions of political power?

12.2 Harsha Vardhana, *The Lady of the Jewel Necklace*, ca. 640 CE

Harsha Vardhana, one of the better known monarchs of India, controlled a wide swath of territory in the northern subcontinent between 606 and 647. Harsha was visited during his reign by the Chinese Buddhist pilgrim Xuan Zang, who described his court and government, and the poet Bana wrote a biography of the king called the *Harshacarita*. However, Harsha himself also wrote at least three plays, two of which were dedicated to the Hindu god Shiva and incorporated actual

Source: Harsha Vardhana, *The Lady of the Jewel Necklace*, trans. Wendy Doniger (New York: NYU Press, 2006), 259–265.

incidents from his court. While the plays are ostensibly fictional, the scene below draws on a real event, reported by Xuan Zang, in which Harsha saved an image of Buddha from a fire that had broken out in his palace. His plays reflect the cosmopolitan and religiously eclectic nature of his court, as well as his view of the status of the advisors and women in his orbit.

KING: (*arising in haste*) What? A fire in the women's quarters? Oh no! What if Queen Vásava datta has been burnt! Oh, my dear Vásava datta!

VÁSAVA·DATTA: Help, my husband, help!

KING: Oh! Why, in my extreme haste and confusion, I didn't notice the queen even though she was standing right here beside me. Courage, my queen, courage!

VÁSAVA·DATTA: My husband, I didn't speak for my own sake. But Ságarika may die, for in my cruelty I had her chained up here. Save her, please, my husband.

KING: What? Ságarika may die, my queen? I will go!

VASU·BHUTI: Your majesty, why should you go the way of a moth for no real reason?

BABHRÁVYA: Your majesty, what Vasu·bhuti said is right.

JESTER: (*grabbing the* KING *by his shirt*) My friend, don't do anything so rash!

KING: (*freeing his shirt*) You idiot! Ságarika may die! Why is the breath of life still in me even now? (*He mimes rushing into the fire and being overcome by smoke.*)

Stop, fire, stop! Give up this unbroken wave
of smoke!
Why do you brandish on high this circling
mass of flames?
If I wasn't burnt up by the fire of separation
from my dear one,
that blazed like the doomsday fire, what can
you do to me?

VÁSAVA·DATTA: Since my husband has unhesitatingly done this because of what I said—miserably unlucky woman that I am—I, too, will follow my husband.

JESTER: (*walking around and standing in front of her*) I, too, ma'am, will be your pathfinder.

VASU·BHUTI: Why, the king of Vatsa has already entered the fire! Then it is proper that I, too, who saw the princess die, should offer myself as an oblation into the fire here.

BABHRÁVYA: Your majesty, why jeopardize the race descended from Bharata for no good reason? But what's the use of idle talk? I too will act in accordance with my devotion.

All mime entering the fire.

Enter SÁGARIKA, *in chains.*

SÁGARIKA: (*looking in all directions*) Oh no! The fire is blazing up on all sides! (*thinking, with satisfaction*) Fortunately, the fire, carrier of oblations, will put an end to my suffering today.

KING: Ságarika is here near the fire! I'll help her right away. (*approaching her in haste*) My dear, how can you remain so self-possessed even now in this haste and confusion?

SÁGARIKA: (*seeing the* KING, *to herself*) Why, it's my husband! When I see him, my love of life comes back again. (*aloud*) Save me, your majesty! Save me!

KING: Don't be afraid, my timid one:

. . .

Clearly the fire does not really burn you,
even though it has caught you,
for your touch now, darling, takes away
even my burning anguish.

. . .

VÁSAVA·DATTA: (*touching the* KING*'s body, with joy*) Thank goodness, my husband's body is unhurt.

KING: This is Babhrávya—

BABHRÁVYA: We've been brought back to life, your majesty.

KING: —and this Vasu·bhuti!—

VASU·BHUTI: Total victory to the great king!

WORKING WITH SOURCES

1. What does the play suggest about Harsha's vision of the ideal relationship between a king and his courtiers?
2. Why was Harsha so careful with stage directions? Did he intend the work to be performed, and how?

12.3 Poetry of the Tang Dynasty, ca. 750 CE

The Tang period (618–907) witnessed a renaissance of poetry, oftentimes compressing vivid natural imagery and poignant emotion into short pieces of only a few verses. The poetry of Li Bo (or Li Bai, 701–762) was particularly influential in the West when his verses on drinking and the pleasures of life were rendered in translation. However, there is also a strong undercurrent of pacifism, drawing on Confucian philosophy, in Tang poetry, and the poems below address war and its consequences. A poem by Du Fu (ca. 721–770), who was also Li Bo's friend, reflects the same sentiment.

Du Fu, "A Drawing of a Horse by General Cao at Secretary Wei Feng's House"

Throughout this dynasty no one had painted horses
Like the master-spirit, Prince Jiangdu—
And then to General Cao through his thirty years of fame
The world's gaze turned, for royal steeds.
He painted the late Emperor's luminous white horse.
For ten days the thunder flew over Dragon Lake,
And a pink-agate plate was sent him from the palace—
The talk of the court-ladies, the marvel of all eyes.
The General danced, receiving it in his honoured home
After this rare gift, followed rapidly fine silks
From many of the nobles, requesting that his art
Lend a new lustre to their screens.
. . . First came the curly-maned horse of Emperor Taizong,
Then, for the Guos, a lion-spotted horse. . . .
But now in this painting I see two horses,
A sobering sight for whosoever knew them.
They are war-horses. Either could face ten thousand.
They make the white silk stretch away into a vast desert.
And the seven others with them are almost as noble
Mist and snow are moving across a cold sky,
And hoofs are cleaving snow-drifts under great trees-
With here a group of officers and there a group of servants.
See how these nine horses all vie with one another—
The high clear glance, the deep firm breath.

. . . Who understands distinction? Who really cares for art?
You, Wei Feng, have followed Cao; Zhidun preceded him.
. . . I remember when the late Emperor came toward his Summer Palace,
The procession, in green-feathered rows, swept from the eastern sky—
Thirty thousand horses, prancing, galloping,
Fashioned, every one of them, like the horses in this picture. . . .
But now the Imperial Ghost receives secret jade from the River God,
For the Emperor hunts crocodiles no longer by the streams.
Where you see his Great Gold Tomb, you may hear among the pines
A bird grieving in the wind that the Emperor's horses are gone.

Li Bo, from *Bright Moon, White Clouds*

Moon over the Pass

Bright moon suddenly *up* from beyond Heaven Mountain,
where it had lain hid in the dark, endless sea of clouds.
The long winds came down tens of thousands of miles,
from the north to blow through Jade Gate Pass.
Here Han troops climbed the road to Paideng Mountain,
because the barbarians wanted our Great Dark Sea in the desert.
Of all who stood upon that ancient field,
I've never heard one returned.
Armed sojourners, they gazed hopelessly
homeward over barren ground,
their hearts gone home: read the bitter faces.
In home's many mansions, facing *this* same moon:
the wives and loved ones also
sigh and see clear, in the mind's eye, yet can't let go.

War South of the Wall

Last year, war:
at the Sang-gan's source.
This year, war:
along the Tsung-ho Road
Our whole army washed weapons in the Tiao-chih Sea,
and set horse to graze on the grass that grew in patches
underneath the snows of the T'ian Shan Range.
Three thousand miles of battles,
three armies exhausted, withering away,
grown old . . .
The Huns farm these battlefields for bones:
since the time of the Ancients, nothing to see
but bleached bones on yellow sands, their fields.
Ch'in built the Wall to keep them out.
Han fed the beacon fires to burn unceasing,
yet the War went on:
war, wasteland: men dying there.
The horses of the conquered neighing skyward, mourning.
Vultures feed on man guts.
With flesh in their beaks they fly up,
fly up to hang those guts in the withered branches.
Soldiers die, blood splashes brush and grass.
Generals?
Is all this done in vain? You know that soldiers
are the direst of instruments. The wise make use of them
only when there is no other way.

WORKING WITH SOURCES

1. What does this poetry suggest about the Confucian and Daoist conceptions of war and its consequences?
2. How do the poems reflect on the preservation of historical memory in monuments and paintings?

12.4 Marco Polo, "Khubilai Khan at War," ca. 1290

Marco Polo (1254–1324) was a member of a clan of Venetian merchants, who had been active in trade in the Middle East for some decades. Polo claims to have accompanied his father and uncle on an extensive trade and diplomatic excursion to China in 1271, and in this account he describes the voyage as well as the people and places he has seen. He further claims to have lived 17 years in China and to have met with, and even served as an official for, Kublai Khan (1215–1294), Genghis Khan's grandson. While some historians have suggested that the account may not be reliable, it demonstrates, at the very least, Western curiosity about Asia and the catalyst of trade in driving some Europeans into hitherto unknown parts of the world.

When the Great Khan had mustered the mere handful of men of which I have spoken, he consulted his astrologers to learn whether he would defeat his enemies and bring his affairs to a happy issue. They assured him that he would deal with his enemies as he pleased. Thereupon he set out with all his forces and went on until after twenty days they came to a great plain where Nayan lay with all his forces, who were not less than 400,000 horsemen. They arrived early in the morning and caught the enemy completely unawares; the Great Khan had had all the roads so carefully watched that no one could come or go without being intercepted, and had thus ensured that the enemy had no suspicion of their approach. Indeed, when they arrived Nayan was in his tent, dallying in bed with his wife, to whom he was greatly attached.

What more shall I say? When the day of battle dawned, the Great Khan suddenly appeared on a mound that rose from the plain where Nayan's forces were bivouacked. They were quite at their ease, like men who had not the faintest suspicion that anyone was approaching with hostile intent. Indeed they felt so secure that they had posted no sentries round their camp and sent out no patrols to van or rear. And suddenly there was the Great Khan on the hill I have mentioned. He stood on the top of a wooden tower, full of crossbowmen and archers, which was carried by four elephants wearing stout leather armour draped with cloths of silk and gold. Above his head flew his banner with the emblem of the sun and moon, so high that it could be clearly seen on every side.

. . .

When Nayan and his men saw the troops of the Great Khan surrounding their camp, they were utterly taken aback. They rushed to arms, arrayed themselves in haste, and formed their ranks in due order.

. . .

So loud was the shouting and the clash of armies that you could not have heard the thunder of heaven. You must know that Nayan was a baptized Christian and in this battle he had the cross of Christ on his standard.

What need to make a long story of it? Enough that this was the most hazardous fight and the most fiercely contested that ever was seen. Never in our time were so many men engaged on one battlefield, especially so many horsemen. So many died on either side that it was a marvel to behold. The battle raged from daybreak till noon, and for a long time its issue hung in the balance; Nayan's followers were so devoted to him, for he was an open-handed master, that they were ready to die rather than turn their backs. But in the end the victory fell to the Great Khan. When

---

Source: Marco Polo, The Travels of Marco Polo, translated with an introduction by Ronald Latham (Penguin Classics, 1958), 115–118.

Nayan and his men saw that they could hold out no longer, they took to flight. But this availed them nothing; for Nayan was taken prisoner, and all his barons and his men surrendered to the Great Khan.

When the Great Khan learnt that Nayan was a prisoner, he commanded that he should be put to death. And this was how it was done. He was wrapped up tightly in a carpet and then dragged about so violently, this way and that, that he died. Their object in choosing this mode of death was so that the blood of the imperial lineage might not be spilt upon the earth, and that sun and air might not witness it.

WORKING WITH SOURCES

1. How did the Great Khan employ elements of "psychological warfare" on the battlefield?
2. Does Marco Polo seem to have felt sympathy for the defeat of a fellow Christian by the non-Christian Khan? Why not?

12.5 Model of a Ming Ship in the Flotilla of Zheng He, ca. 1420

Between 1405 and 1433, a series of naval expeditions were sent out by Yongle, the third emperor of the Ming Dynasty, under the command of the remarkable Zheng He (1371–1435). The largest of Zheng's ships were over 400 feet long and were thus more than four times the length of Christopher Columbus's *Santa Maria*. His voyages took Zheng to the coasts of southeast Asia, Indonesia, India, Arabia, and East Africa. In 2010, marine archaeologists attempted to find remains of one of Zheng's ships off the coast of Kenya, near Malindi, a site Zheng visited in 1418. This photograph shows a model of one of Zheng's ships, compared with a model of the *Santa Maria*. The model is displayed in a shopping mall in Dubai, United Arab Emirates.

Source: © Liu Liqun/ChinaStock

WORKING WITH SOURCES

1. What does the greater size of Zheng He's ships compared to the ones Columbus used say about the imperial ambitions of Ming China in the fifteenth century?
2. Why might this ship be of interest to shoppers in Dubai?

13. RELIGIOUS CIVILIZATIONS INTERACTING: KOREA, JAPAN, AND VIETNAM, 550–1500 CE

13.1 Murasaki Shikibu, *The Tale of Genji*, ca. 1000

The daughter of a minor noble in the court at Heian-Kyo in central Japan, Murasaki Shikibu (ca. 973–1025) created Japan's most popular work of fiction and one of the world's great literary masterpieces. *The Tale of Genji (Genji Monagatori)* is composed of acute observations of the subtleties of court life, and Murasaki focused particularly on the lives of women at court. Although the tale is ostensibly fictional, it reflects the era in which it was written, as the novelist strove to make the action in it plausible to the reader. In the process, she also crafted a compelling and compulsively readable story.

When he [Genji] returned to His Excellency's residence, sleep eluded him. Images of her [the Rokujō Haven, his love interest] as he had known her down the years ran through his mind, and he wondered in vain regret why she had taken such offense at each of his casual diversions, undertaken while he complacently assumed that she would eventually change her mind about him, and why she had persisted to the end in disliking him so. It seemed like a dream now to be wearing gray, and the thought that her gray would have been still darker if she had outlived him prompted,

> I may do no more, and the mourning I now wear is a shallow gray, but my tears upon my sleeves have gathered in deep pools.

He went on to call the Buddha's Name, looking more beautiful than ever, and his discreet chanting of the scripture passage, "O **Lord Fugen** who seest all the manifest universe," outdid the most practiced monk's. The sight of his little son would start fresh tears for "the grasses of remembering" and yet without this reminder of her. . . . The thought gave him some comfort.

. . .

He now held the world and its ways, so distasteful already, in unqualified aversion, and he thought that without this fresh tie he would certainly assume the guise to which he aspired, except that every time his mind took this turn, he would straightaway start thinking how much his young lady in the west wing must miss him. He still felt a void beside him, however closely his women might gather around him while he lay at night alone in his curtained bed. Often he lay wakeful, murmuring, "Is autumn the time to lose one's love?" and listening, sick at heart, to the priests, whom he had chosen for their voices, calling the name of the Buddha Amida.

Oh, how sadly the wind moans as autumn passes! he thought as for once he lay alone and sleepless into a foggy dawn, but then a letter arrived on deep blue-gray paper, tied to chrysanthemums just now beginning to open and placed beside him by a messenger who left without a word. The delightful effect pleased him, and he noted that the writing was the Haven's.

Lord Fugen: A Bodhisattva closely associated with the Lotus Sutra.

Source: Murasaki Shikibu, The Tale of Genji, translated by Royall Tyler (Penguin, 2001), 178–179.

"Have you understood my silence?

The sad news I hear, that a life can pass so soon,
brings tears to my eyes,
but my thoughts go first of all to the sleeves of the
bereaved.

My heart is so full, you know, beneath this sky."

Her writing is more beautiful than ever! He could hardly put it down, but her pretense of innocence repelled him. Still, he had not the heart to withhold an answer, and he hated to imagine the damage to her name if he should do so. Perhaps the lady he had lost had indeed been destined somehow to meet this end, but why should he have seen and heard the cause so clearly? Yes, he was bitter, and despite himself he did not think that he could ever feel the same about the Haven again.

After long hesitation, since the Ise Priestess's purification might well present another difficulty, he decided that it would be cruel not to answer a letter so pointedly sent, and he wrote on mauve-gray paper, "My own silence has indeed lasted too long, but although I have thought of you, I knew that in this time of mourning you would understand."

WORKING WITH SOURCES

1. What view of Japanese court life in the Heian period is revealed in this passage? How do the requirements of place, name, reputation, and hierarchy create tension for Genji?
2. What does the passage suggest about the religious beliefs and syncretism of Japanese society in this period?

13.2 *Haedong kosŭng chŏn*, on Buddhism in Korea, ca. 1215

The *Lives of Eminent Korean Monks* is a compilation of biographies of Buddhist monks from the Three Kingdoms period of Korean history (first century BCE through the tenth century CE). It promotes Buddhist piety by stressing the (often supernatural) deeds of these monks, and it is also a valuable source for Korean history. In spite of its importance, the work was long thought lost until portions of it were found at a Buddhist temple in the early twentieth century. This passage of the *Lives* deals with the introduction of Buddhism as the national faith of the Silla Kingdom in 527 CE, under King Pŏpkong.

The monk Pŏpkong was the twenty-third king of Silla, Pŏphŭng [514–540]. His secular name was Wŏnjong; he was the first son of King Chijŭng [500–514] and Lady Yŏnje. He was seven feet tall. Generous, he loved the people, and they in turn regarded him as a saint or a sage. Millions of people, therefore, placed confidence in him. In the third year [516] a dragon appeared in the Willow Well. In the fourth year [517] the Ministry of War was established, and in the seventh year [520] laws and statutes were promulgated together with the official vestments. After his enthronement, whenever the king attempted to spread Buddhism his ministers opposed him with much dispute. He felt frustrated, but, remembering Ado's devout vow, he summoned all his officials and said to them: "Our august ancestor, King Mich'u, together with Ado, propagated

Source: "Pŏpkong Declares Buddhism the National Faith," in Peter H. Lee, ed. *Sourcebook of Korean Civilization*, vol. 1, *From Early Times to the Sixteenth Century* (New York: Columbia University Press, 1993), 75–77.

Buddhism, but he died before great merits were accumulated. That the knowledge of the wonderful transformation of śākyamuni should be prevented from spreading makes me very sad. We think we ought to erect monasteries and recast images to continue our ancestor's fervor. What do you think?" Minister Kongal and others remonstrated with the king, saying, "In recent years the crops have been scarce, and the people are restless. Besides, because of frequent border raids from the neighboring state, our soldiers are still engaged in battle. How can we exhort our people to erect a useless building at this time?" The king, depressed at the lack of faith among his subordinates, sighed, saying, "We, lacking moral power, are unworthy of succeeding to the throne. The yin and the yang are disharmonious and the people ill at ease; therefore you opposed my idea and did not want to follow. Who can enlighten the strayed people by the wonderful dharma?" For some time no one answered.

In the fourteenth year [527] the Grand Secretary Pak Yŏmch'ok (Ich'adon or Kŏch'adon), then twenty-six years old, was an upright man. With a heart that was sincere and deep, he advanced resolutely for the righteous cause. Out of willingness to help the king fulfill his noble vow, he secretly memorialized the throne: "If Your Majesty desires to establish Buddhism, may I ask Your Majesty to pass a false decree to this officer that the king desires to initiate Buddhist activities? Once the ministers learn of this, they will undoubtedly remonstrate. Your Majesty, declaring that no such decree has been given, will then ask who has forged the royal order. They will ask Your Majesty to punish my crime, and if their request is granted, they will submit to Your Majesty's will."

The king said, "Since they are bigoted and haughty, we fear they will not be satisfied even with your execution." Yŏmch'ok replied, "Even the deities venerate the religion of the Great Sage. If an officer as unworthy as myself is killed for its cause, miracles must happen between heaven and earth. If so, who then will dare to remain bigoted and haughty?" The king answered, "Our basic wish is to further the advantageous and remove the disadvantageous. But now we have to injure a loyal subject. Is this not sorrowful?" Yŏmch'ok replied, "Sacrificing his life in order to accomplish goodness is the great principle of the official. Moreover, if it means the eternal brightness of the Buddha Sun and the perpetual solidarity of the kingdom, the day of my death will be the year of my birth." The king, greatly moved, praised Yŏmch'ok and said, "Though you are a commoner, your mind harbors thoughts worthy of brocaded and embroidered robes." Thereupon the king and Yŏmch'ok vowed to be true to each other.

Afterward a royal decree was issued, ordering the erection of a monastery in the Forest of the Heavenly Mirror, and officials in charge began construction. The court officials, as expected, denounced it and expostulated with the king. The king remarked, "We did not issue such an order." Thereupon Yŏmch'ok spoke out, "Indeed, I did this purposely, for if we practice Buddhism the whole country will become prosperous and peaceful. As long as it is good for the administration of the realm, what wrong can there be in forging a decree?" Thereupon, the king called a meeting and asked the opinion of the officials. All of them remarked, "These days monks bare their heads and wear strange garments. Their discourses are wrong and in violation of the Norm. If we unthinkingly follow their proposals, there may be cause for regret. We dare not obey Your Majesty's order, even if we are threatened with death." Yŏmch'ok spoke with indignation, saying, "All of you are wrong, for there must be an unusual personage before there can be an unusual undertaking. I have heard that the teaching of Buddhism is profound and arcane. We must practice it. How can a sparrow know the great ambition of a swan?" The king said, "The will of the majority is firm and unalterable. You are the only one who takes a different view. I cannot follow two recommendations at the same time." He then ordered the execution of Yŏmch'ok.

WORKING WITH SOURCES

1. What does Yŏmch'ok's plan reveal about resistance to Buddhism in Korea in the sixth century—and about the role of an advisor to the Korean king in the period?
2. What seems to have been the role of self-sacrifice in the establishment of Buddhism in Korea?

13.3 *Nihongi Shoki (Chronicles of Japan)*, ca. 720 CE

The *Nihongi Shoki* is the first official history of Japan. It draws on numerous sources, including Chinese histories, clan histories, and the accounts of religious authorities. While it parallels the *Kojiki* in describing the ancient and mythological origins of Japan, it continues the narrative far beyond the *Kojiki* into the recent past, specifically the reign of the Empress Jitō (686–697). This particular story concerns the eleventh emperor of Japan, Suinin, but it differs from the *Kojiki* in certain key details, and probably reflects the values of the eighth century rather than its ostensible setting (the first century CE).

Fourth year, autumn, Ninth Month, twenty-third day. The empress's elder maternal brother, Prince Sahobiko, plotted treason and tried to endanger the state. He watched for an occasion when the empress was enjoying her leisure and addressed her as follows: "Whom do you love best—your elder brother or your husband?"

At this, the empress, ignorant of his object in making this inquiry, immediately answered, saying: "I love my elder brother." Then he enticed the empress by saying: "If one serves a man by beauty, when the beauty fades, his affection will cease. . . . I beg you, therefore, to slay the emperor for me." So he took a dagger and, giving it to the empress, said: "Put on this dagger with your garments, and when the emperor goes to sleep, stab him in the neck and kill him."

. . .

Fifth year, winter, Tenth Month, first day. The emperor proceeded to Kume, where he dwelled in Takamiya. Now the emperor took his noon-day nap with the empress's knees as his pillow. Up to this time the empress had done nothing but thought vainly to herself: "This would be the time to do what the prince, my elder brother, plotted." And she wept tears which fell on the emperor's face.

The emperor woke and addressed the empress, saying: "Today we have had a dream. A small brocade-color snake coiled itself around our neck and a great rain arose from Saho, which coming here wet our faces. What does this portend?" At this the empress, knowing that she could not conceal the plot, in fear and awe bowed to the earth and informed the emperor fully of the circumstances of the prince's, her elder brother's, treason.

. . .

Then the emperor addressed the empress, saying: "This is not your crime," and raising a force from the neighboring district, he commanded Yatsunada, the remote ancestor of the Kimi of Kōzuke, to slay Sahobiko. Now Sahobiko withstood him with an army, and, hastily piling up rice stalks, made a castle, which was so solid that it could not be breached. This is what was called a "rice castle." A month passed, and yet it did not surrender.

The empress grieved at this, saying: "Even though I am empress, with what countenance can I preside over the empire, after bringing to ruin the prince, my elder brother?" Accordingly, she took in her arms the imperial prince Homutsu-wake and entered the rice castle of the prince, her elder brother. The emperor increased his army still more and, having surrounded the castle on all sides, proclaimed to those inside, saying: "Send forth quickly the empress and the imperial prince." But they would not send them out. So General Yatsunada set fire to the castle. Then the empress, taking in her bosom the imperial child, crossed the castle and came out.

Immediately she sought the emperor saying: "The reason why your handmaiden at first fled into her elder brother's castle was in the hope that her elder brother

---

Source: "The Empress and Her Brother Prince Sahobiko," from *Traditional Japanese Literature: An Anthology, Beginnings to 1600*, ed. Haruo Shirane (New York: Columbia University Press, 2007), 47–49.

might be absolved from guilt for the sake of her and her child. But now he has not been absolved, and I know that I am guilty. Shall I have my hands tied behind my back? There is nothing left but for me to strangle myself. But even though I, your handmaiden, die, I cannot bear to forget the favor shown me by the emperor. I pray, therefore, that the empress's palace, which I had charge of, may be granted to consorts for you. In the land of Tanba there are five ladies, all of virtuous minds, the daughters of the prince, who is Michi no Ushi of Tanba. Let them be placed in the side courts to complete the number of the consort chambers." To this the emperor agreed. Then the fire blazed up, and the castle was destroyed. All the troops ran away, and Sahobiko and his younger sister died together inside the castle. Thereupon the emperor commended the good service of General Yatsunada and granted him the name of Yamato-hi-muke-hiko Yatsunada.

WORKING WITH SOURCES

1. Contrast the emperor's reactions to his wife in the two episodes. What do these differences reveal about Japanese culture?
2. What does the document suggest about women's familial roles and expectations for their behavior?

13.4 P'i Jih-hsiu, "Three Poems of Shame," ca. 865 CE

Because there are very few sources of information on the history of Vietnam before the Li dynasty (1010–1225), Chinese dynastic histories and Chinese poetry are indispensable sources. They are valuable even when, as in this case, they were composed by those on the other side of conflict with Vietnamese insurgents. P'i Jih-hsiu was a prominent Tang poet of the late ninth century, and he was particularly drawn to the Mencian notion that the people have the right to revolt if their country is being mismanaged. While traveling through the country in 865, he stopped in the city of Hsü, from which 2,000 men had been drafted for the Tang army and sent to fight Nan-chao in Vietnam. These soldiers were probably lost when Nan-chao defeated the Chinese forces in Vietnam in early 863, and news of their defeat apparently reached Hsü while Jih-hsiu was there.

The south was neglected, officials were not
    selected,
Causing the overthrow of our Giao-chi,
Which, for three or four successive years,
Has drifted away, bringing disgrace to the empire.
The timid yield readily in battle;
The warlike revel in their weapons.
Soldiers fill the empire,
Battle leaders accumulate treasure;
Exactions reduce the common people to misery,
In order to distribute the wages of valiant men.
Brave Hsü-ch'ang warriors,
Their loyalty and daring brought honor to their
    families;
They went with the wind of myriad galloping
    horses,

Source: Keith Weller Taylor, *The Birth of Vietnam* (Berkeley: University of California Press, 1983), 345–346.

They ceased in a river of flesh.
Yesterday morning the defeated troops returned;
There is weeping at a thousand gates and ten thousand hearths.
The sound of wailing echoes through the village streets;
Resentment spreads over the mountains and valleys.
Who can listen to wardrums in the daytime,
And not suffer the sight of metal arrowheads?
I have a plan for victory,
Though irregular and considered worthless by others.
I store it in my mind and heart;
I am ashamed to see the families of the Hsü warriors.
I lament those thoughtless ones,
Who simply follow the steps of their ancestors.
My family does not produce grain for the army;
I am not familiar with military affairs.
Yet I wear the same kind of clothing as the Hsü warriors,
And I eat the same kind of food as the Hsü warriors.
Now I know that the teachings of the Ancients
Are already enough to shelter me.
To whose shame is this song sung?
The Ying River flows far and green.

WORKING WITH SOURCES

1. Can this poem be compared with other T'ang poetry regarding pacifism and war?
2. What does the poem indicate about the growth of a national identity and culture in Vietnam?

13.5 Copper Head of Bodhisattva Avalokiteshvara, Vietnam, Eighth–Ninth Century CE

This head, crafted from copper alloy, is all that remains of an impressive image found in central Vietnam. It depicts the Avalokiteshvara, the embodiment of Buddhist compassion, and the Amitabha Buddha is perched on the crown. It points to the emergence of a pan–southeast Asian bodhisattva type in the eighth and ninth centuries, as well as to the superb metal-casting skills of artisans in the Cham territories of Vietnam.

Source: Photo: Thierry Ollivier. © RMN-Grand Palais/Art Resource, NY

WORKING WITH SOURCES

1. How does the image reveal the phenomenon of "religious civilizations interacting" and the emergence of an international Buddhist culture in Southeast Asia?
2. What does the head suggest about the social structure of Vietnam in this period?

14. PATTERNS OF STATE FORMATION IN AFRICA, 600–1450 CE

14.1 The Fetha Nagast, Ethiopia, Fifteenth Century

In the medieval period Ethiopia became a multiethnic, multilingual, and multireligious state in which the kings limited the church's conversion efforts. Nevertheless, the kings continued to emphasize their Christian identity, and this factor is reflected in their adoption and endorsement of the Fetha Nagast, or Law of the Kings, in the mid-fifteenth century. This legal code had originally been written in Arabic by a Coptic Christian in Egypt, probably in the mid-thirteenth century. While living under Muslim rule, the Copts were allowed to adopt portions of Justinian's law code and the resolutions of church councils for their own governance. Translated from Greek, and with many Biblical passages added, the code connected Egyptian Christians to their Byzantine, Roman, and Judeo-Christian heritage, founding the basis of law squarely in that tradition. The Ethiopian monarchs had the Arabic source translated into Ge'ez (the state language of Ethiopia at the time), and the translator added a section on kingship, a portion of which is offered below. The Law of the Kings remained the law in Ethiopia until 1930, when Emperor Haile Selassie I issued the country's first modern constitution.

CHAPTER XLIV, KINGS

SECTION I

TH. The king you appoint must be one of your brethren. It is not proper for you to appoint over yourself an alien and an infidel, lest he multiply horses, women, gold and silver [to himself]. And when he sits on the throne of his kingdom, some priests shall write for him the Divine Book, so that he may keep it by his side and read it throughout his life, in order to learn the fear of God, his Creator, to observe his commandments, and to practice them, lest his heart become proud [and feel contempt] for his brethren. He must never swerve either to the right or to the left from what has been laid down in the Law, so that his days and his sons' days may be prolonged in his kingdom [Deuteronomy 17:15f], and his faith in God may be perfect. **EB 9.** Because of faith the walls of Jericho were pulled down, when the sons of Israel marched around them for seven days. Because of faith, Gideon and Barak and Samson and Jephtha and David defeated the kings, served the cause of justice, found what they hoped for, were victors in war, and defeated the army of the enemy [Hebrews 11:30, 32f]. **RSTA 54.** And if the king becomes a heretic, from that moment he is no longer a king, but a rebel.

SECTION II

Our Lord said in the Gospel: "Give to the king what is the king's and to God what is God's [Matthew 22:21]." And Apostle Paul said in his letter to the Romans: "Every one of you must be submissive to the authority of your ruler, since a ruler is appointed only by God. And God has appointed all these rulers. . . ." [Romans 13:1f]

Source: Excerpt from *The Fetha Nagast*, trans. Paulos Tzadua, ed. Peter L. Strauss (Durham, NC: Carolina Academic Press, 2009), 271–273.

St. John Chrysostom, in his explanation of this passage, has said: "The Apostle had already shown [this] in his other letters, commanding the [lesser] chiefs to give due obedience to the higher chiefs, as the servant must obey the master. This the Apostle did, showing that Our Lord did not abrogate all the laws by His precepts, but confirmed them. And his saying: "Every soul" is because every man must conform himself to this; and his saying: "A ruler is appointed only by God," means that God has provided for the appointment of judges and rulers to take place, so that the world may become beautifully calm. And for that reason He has established the ruler, since equality of forces causes many wars. And God in His wisdom has established many kinds of authority, such as that of a man in respect to woman, the father in respect to the son, the old in respect to the young, the master in respect to the slave, the teacher in respect to the disciple, and, more so, the chief in respect to the one who is placed under him. The Lord acted in the same manner with the body, [creating] the head and placing the other parts under it; he also did thus with other animals, such as bees, ***raza***, ants, antelopes, eagles, buffaloes, and all kinds of fish—every one has its chief, and when there is no authority there is confusion and lack of order. And his words: "Since he is God's minister calling thee to good and beautiful things," mean that he will lead you daily in your obedience to God. His punishments will be directed against those who rebel against God, murderers, fornicators, thieves, and wrong-doers; but his favors go to the obedient, who obey the Highest—Whose name be praised!—to those who despite the world and to those who do works of perfection and are righteous.

. . .

Raza: A type of bird.

SECTION III

MAK 37. Let the king give honor to the order of the clergy, as Constantine, elected, faithful, and righteous king, and those who were after him did. Let him give from his wealth to each of them, according to their rank. First of all he shall give to the bishops, then to the priests, next, to the deacons, and then to those who are below them. He shall exempt them from tribute, presents, and the other things to be given to the rulers. Let him assign something to the churches for the maintenance of widows, orphans, and the poor, so that they may entreat God to strengthen the true faith with belief in the Holy Trinity, so that the day of the Christians' king may be long.

. . .

SECTION IV

The king shall judge with equity in the middle of his people. He shall not be partial, either toward himself or toward the others, toward his son, his relatives, his friends, or the alien in any way which brings about injustice. And it is written in reference to kings: "The honored king loves justice, but the unjust king loves evil and injustice, to the ruin of his soul." And Solomon the wise has said: "To increase justice and save the oppressed is better than the offering and sacrifices" [Proverbs 21:3]

Do not take the wealth of anyone by violence; do not buy from him by force, either openly or by trick, in order not to be afflicted by God in this world and in the future. In this world, as befell the King Ahab and his wife Jezebel, when Naboth refused to sell him his vineyard and Jezebel schemed to kill him and took the vineyard; God smote Ahab and made his race perish; and next to him he smote Jezebel, and the dogs ate her in the aforesaid vineyard [2 Kings 21]. As for the future world, the Apostle said: "Wrong-doers and apostates shall not inherit God's Kingdom" [1 Corinthians 6:9]

WORKING WITH SOURCES

1. How does the author of this portion of the Fetha Nagast use Biblical passages and historical comparisons to accentuate his points? Why?
2. What is the king's primary obligation to his people? Under what conditions could he lose his power?

14.2 Ibn Battuta on Mali, from the *Rihla*, ca. 1354

One of the great world travelers of all time, Ibn Battuta was an educated Moroccan who journeyed throughout Africa, the Middle East, Persia, and Asia. In 1354, at age 50, Ibn Battuta dictated an account of his travels, the *Rihla* (the *Journey*), to Ibn Juzayy, a court secretary in Morocco. Both men therefore had a role to play in shaping the narrative.

I set out on the 1st Muharram of the year seven hundred and fifty-three (18 February, 1352 CE) with a caravan including amongst others a number of the merchants of Sijilmasa [present day Morocco/Algerian frontier region]. After twenty-five days we reached Taghaza, an unattractive village, with the curious feature that its houses and mosques are built of blocks of salt, roofed with camel skins. There are no trees there, nothing but sand. In the sand is a salt mine; they dig for the salt, and find it in thick slabs, lying one on top of the other, as though they had been tool-squared and laid under the surface of the earth. A camel will carry two of these slabs. No one lives at Taghaza except the slaves of the Masufa tribe, who dig for the salt; they subsist on dates imported from Dara and Sijilmasa, camel's flesh, and millet imported from the Negrolands. The Negroes come up from their country and take away the salt from there. At Walata a load of salt brings eight to ten mithqals; in the town of Mali it sells for twenty to thirty, and sometimes as much as forty. The Negroes use salt as a medium of exchange, just as gold and silver is used elsewhere; they cut it up into pieces and buy and sell with it. The business done at Taghaza, for all its meanness, amounts to an enormous figure in terms of hundredweights of gold dust. . . .

Thus we reached the town of Walata after a journey of two months to a day. Walata is the northernmost province of the Negroes, and the Sultan's representative there was one Farba Husayn, Farba meaning deputy (in their language). . . .

It was an excessively hot place, and boasts a few small date-palms, in the shade of which they sow watermelons. Its water comes from underground water beds at that point, and there is plenty of mutton to be had. The garments of the inhabitants, most of whom belong to the Masufa tribe, are of fine Egyptian fabrics. Their women are of surpassing beauty, and are shown more respect than the men. The state of affairs amongst these people is indeed extraordinary. Their men show no sign of jealousy whatever; no one claims descent from his father, but on the contrary from his mother's brother. A person's heirs are his sister's sons, not his own sons. This is a thing which I have seen nowhere in the world except among the Indians of Malabar. But those are heathens; these people are Muslims, punctilious in observing the hours of prayer, studying books of law, and memorizing the Koran. Yet their women show no bashfulness before men and do not veil themselves, though they are assiduous in attending prayers. Any man who wishes to marry one of them may do so, they do not travel with their husbands. . . .

The women have their "friends" and "companions" amongst the men outside their own families, and the men in the same way have "companions" amongst the women of other families. A man may go into his house and find his wife entertaining her "companion," but he takes not objection to it. One day at Walata I went into the ***qadi's*** house, after asking his permission to enter, and found with a young woman of remarkable beauty. When I saw her I was shocked and turned to go out, but she laughed at me, instead of being overcome by shame, and the quadi

Qadi: A Muslim judge.

Source: Ibn Battuta, "Mali," from *Travels in Asia and Africa, 1325–1354*, trans. and ed. H. A. R. Gibb (New York: Robert M. McBride, 1929), 323–327, 329–330.

said to me, "Why are you going out? She is my companion." I was amazed at their conduct, for he was a theologian and a pilgrim to boot. I was told that he had asked the sultan's permission to make the pilgrimage that year with his "companion" (whether this one or not I cannot say) but the sultan would not grant it.

. . . On feast-days, after Dugha [interpreter] has finished his display, the poets come in. Each of them is inside a figure resembling a thrush, made of feathers, and provided with a wooden head with a red beak, to look like a thrush's head. They stand in front of the sultan in this ridiculous make-up and recite their poems. I was told that their poetry is a kind of sermonizing in which they say to the sultan: "This pempi [throne] which you occupy was that whereon sat this king and that king, and such were this one's noble actions and such and such the other's. So do you too do good deeds whose memory will outlive you." After that the chief of the poets mounts the steps of the pempi and lays hid head on the sultan's lap, then climbs to the top of the pempi and lays his head on first on the sultan's right shoulder and then on his left, speaking all the while in their tongue, and finally he comes down again. I was told that this practice is a very old custom amongst them prior to the introduction of Islam, and they have kept it up.

. . . The Negroes possess some admirable qualities. They are seldom unjust, and have a greater abhorrence of injustice than any other people. The sultan shows no mercy to anyone who is guilty of the least act of it. There is a complete security in their country. Neither traveler nor inhabitant in it has anything to fear from robbers or men of violence. They do not confiscate the property of any white man [Arab trader] who dies in their country, even if it be accounted wealth. On the contrary, they give it into the charge of some trustworthy person among the whites, until the rightful heir takes possession of it. They are careful to observe the hours of prayer, and assiduous in attending them in congregations, and in bringing up their children to them. On Fridays, if a man does not go early to the mosque, he cannot find a corner to pray in, on account of the crowd. It is a custom of theirs to send each man his boy (to the mosque) with his prayer-mat; the boy spreads it out for his master in a place befitting him and remains on it (until his master comes to the mosque). The pray-mats are made of the leaves of a tree resembling a date-palm, but without fruit.

Another of their good qualities is their habit of wearing clean white garments on Fridays. Even if a man has nothing but an old worn shirt, he washes it and cleans it, and wears it at the Friday service. Yet another is their zeal for learning the Koran by heart. They put their children in chains if they show any backwardness in memorizing it, and they are not set free until they have it by heart. I visited the qadi in his house on the day of the festival. His children were chained up, so I said to him, "Will you not let them loose?" He replied, "I shall not do so until they learn the Koran by heart." Among their bad qualities are the following. The women servants, slave-girls, and young girls go about in front of everyone naked, without a stitch of clothing on them. Women go into the sultan's presence naked and without coverings, and his daughters also go about naked. Then there is the custom of their putting dust and ashes on their heads as a mark of respect, and the grotesque ceremonies we have described when the poets recite their verses.

WORKING WITH SOURCES

1. Why does Ibn Battuta remark so often on the lack of generosity on the part of the sultan of Mali?
2. Ibn Battuta offers many details about the material culture of Mali. What does his description reveal about the interactions between Mali and other cultures? How do they interact?

14.3 Golden Bracelets from the "Lost City" of Mapungubwe, South Africa, Thirteenth Century

The archaeological site of Mapungubwe, first discovered and excavated in the 1930s, spans the borders of present-day South Africa, Zimbabwe, and Botswana. It was one of the most powerful African Iron Age states, dominating southern Africa from 1070 to 1300 and establishing trade contacts with the Middle East and India. The source of its influence was the gold mined in the territory, fashioned into objects, and then exported far beyond the borders of the kingdom.

WORKING WITH SOURCES

1. How do these items crafted from gold illustrate the sophistication of Mapungubwe culture, as well as its desire to display wealth?
2. Might these particular items have been related to the social structure of Mapungubwe, and particularly to the role of royal wives?

Source: University of Pretoria Museums, South Africa, Mapungubwe Collection, copyright University of Pretoria.

14.4 'Abd al-'Azīz al-Bakrī, *Description of Northern Africa*, 1068

Al-Bakrī was born in Spain, and it appears that he never left that country. However, he collected information from people he met who had traveled to the Sahara and the Sudan, and he published his findings in a work called *The Book of Routes and Realms* (*Kitāb al-masālik wa-'l-mamālik*). Al-Bakrī, who died in 1094, was famous for his curiosity about the geography, languages, and natural landscape of places he had not himself visited. The greater part of his major book is still unpublished, but the following section provides insight into the changing religious landscape in Ghana in the early eleventh century.

GHĀNA AND THE CUSTOMS OF ITS INHABITANTS

Ghāna is a title given to their kings; the name of the region is Awkār, and their king today, namely in the year 460/ 1067–8, is Tunkā Manīn. He ascended the throne in 455/ 1063. The name of his predecessor was Basī and he became their ruler at the age of 85. He led a praiseworthy life on account of his love of justice and friendship for the Muslims. At the end of his life he became blind, but he concealed this from his subjects and pretended that he could see. When something was put before him he said: "This is good" or "This is bad." His ministers deceived the people by indicating to the king in cryptic words what he should say, so that the commoners could not understand.

. . .

The city of Ghāna consists of two towns situated on a plain. One of these towns, which is inhabited by Muslims, is large and possesses twelve mosques, in one of which they assemble for the Friday prayer. There are salaried imams and muezzins, as well as jurists and scholars. In the environs are wells with sweet water, from which they drink and with which they grow vegetables. The king's town is six miles distant from this one and bears the name of Al-Ghā ba. Between these two towns there are continuous habitations. The houses of the inhabitants are of stone and acacia (*sunt*) wood. The king has a palace and a number of domed dwellings all surrounded with an enclosure like a city wall (*sūr*). In the king's town, and not far from his court of justice, is a mosque where the Muslims who arrive at his court (*yafid 'alayh*) pray. Around the king's town are domed buildings and groves and thickets where the sorcerers of these people, men in charge of the religious cult, live. In them too are their idols and the tombs of their kings. These woods are guarded and none may enter them and know what is there. In them also are the king's prisons. If somebody is imprisoned there no news of him is ever heard. The king's interpreters, the official in charge of his treasury and the majority of his ministers are Muslims. Among the people who follow the king's religion only he and his heir apparent (who is the son of his sister) may wear sewn clothes. All other people wear robes of cotton, silk, or brocade, according to their means. All of them shave their beards, and women shave their heads.

. . .

When the people who profess the same religion as the king approach him they fall on their knees and sprinkle dust on their heads, for this is their way of

Source: 'Abd al-'Azīz al-Bakrī, Description of Northern Africa, on "Ghāna and the customs of its inhabitants," in N. Levtzion and J. F. P. Hopkins, *Corpus of early Arabic sources for West African history* (Cambridge, 1981), translated by J. F. P. Hopkins, pp. 79–81.

greeting him. As for the Muslims, they greet him only by clapping their hands.

Their religion is paganism and the worship of idols (*dakākīr*). When their king dies they construct over the place where his tomb will be an enormous dome of *sāj* [teak?] wood. Then they bring him on a bed covered with a few carpets and cushions and place him beside the dome. At his side they place his ornaments, his weapons, and the vessels from which he used to eat and drink, filled with various kinds of food and beverages. They place there too the men who used to serve his meals. They close the door of the dome and cover it with mats and furnishings. Then the people assemble, who heap earth upon it until it becomes like a big hillock and dig a ditch around it until the mound can be reached at only one place.

WORKING WITH SOURCES

1. Is there anything surprising, at least in al-Bakrī's description, in the reinforcement of royal authority in Ghana?
2. How was the religious balance between Muslims and non-Muslims maintained in this kingdom, and why?

14.5 Walls and Moats at Sungbo's Eredo, Nigeria, ca. 1000–1450

The chiefdom of Ijebu encompassed a capital and villages on a territory of 22 square miles, surrounded by a deep moat and towering rampart almost 100 miles long. The iron-saturated soil would have made the construction process very difficult, especially since the labor was achieved with nothing more than iron shovels. This line drawing illustrates what archaeologists believe to have been the arrangement of a typical cross section of this structure. It is named for Bilikisu Sungo, a mythical priestess-queen who was credited with ordering the construction of the moat and rampart.

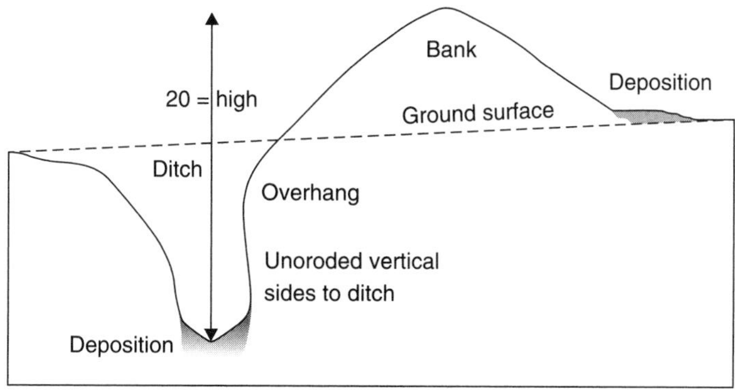

Source: By Nyame Akuma, 1998.

WORKING WITH SOURCES

1. Was this moat and rampart constructed for defensive purposes, or for some other reason? How do the size and extent of walls and moats of Ijebu compare with defensive structures created by other civilizations in the period before 1500 CE?
2. What does the existence of this edifice reveal about the use of collective labor in Ijebu in this period?

15. THE RISE OF EMPIRES IN THE AMERICAS, 600–1550 CE

15.1 The Temple of the Jaguars, Chichén Itzá, ca. 850–1000 CE

Chichén Itzá was founded during a period of renewed urbanization in the Mayan states around 650, and a remarkable state flourished in its vicinity between 850 and 1000. The population was composed of local Maya, as well as Maya-speaking peoples from the Gulf of Mexico coast. It owed its prosperity to long-distance trade, both overland and in boats along the coast. Around 1000, the ruling-class factions abandoned Chichén Itzá for unknown reasons, and the city-state dwindled in size to the level of a town.

Dreamstime/© Alexandre Fagundes De Fagundes (above); Shutterstock/Danilo Ascione (on next page)

WORKING WITH SOURCES

1. What does the construction of this monument suggest about the social structure of Chichén Itzá at its height?
2. What might have been the significance of the jaguars? Why would the temple have been decorated in such an elaborate fashion?

15.2 Skeletons in a Wari Royal Tomb Site, El Castillo de Huarmey, Peru, ca. 600–1000 CE

In 2013, 63 skeletons were discovered in a tomb at El Castillo de Huarmey, about 175 miles north of Lima, in what would seem to be the first imperial tomb of the Wari culture discovered in modern times. Most of the bodies were female, and wrapped in bundles in a seated position typical of Wari burials. Three of the women appear to have been Wari queens, as they were buried

Source: REUTERS/Enrique Castro-Mendivil.

with gold and silver jewelry and brilliantly painted ceramics. However, six of the skeletons were not wrapped in the textiles, but instead positioned on top of the burials. Archaeologists have concluded that these people may have been sacrificed for the benefit of the others.

WORKING WITH SOURCES

1. How do the burial practices of Wari culture compare with those of other civilizations in Mesoamerica and the Andes?
2. What might this tomb suggest about the roles and expectations of women in Wari culture?

15.3 Bernal Díaz, *The Conquest of New Spain*, ca. 1568

In the course of the fifteenth century, the Aztecs established an empire centered in the Valley of Mexico (surrounding present-day Mexico City, after the drainage of most of the valley) but encompassing Mesoamerica from the Pacific to the Gulf of Mexico. The resulting state, far more

Source: The Conquest of New Spain, translated with an introduction by J. M. Cohen (Penguin Classics, 1963), pp. 232–234.

centralized than the preceding Teotihuacán and Toltec city-states, commanded a large extent of territory and thrived on the trade in raw materials that were brought in from both coasts of their empire. Bernal Díaz, born in 1492 in Spain, would join the Spaniards in the "conquest" of Mexico, but he also left behind vivid eyewitness accounts of occupied Aztec society in the sixteenth century. Among them is this description of the market in Tlatelolco, one of the central cities at the heart of Aztec imperial power.

Our Captain and those of us who had horses went to Tlatelolco mounted, and the majority of our men were fully equipped. On reaching the market-place, escorted by the many ***Caciques*** whom Montezuma had assigned to us, we were astounded at the great number of people and the quantities of merchandise, and at the orderliness and good arrangements that prevailed, for we had never seen such a thing before. The chieftains who accompanied us pointed everything out. Every kind of merchandise was kept separate and had its fixed place marked for it.

Let us begin with the dealers in gold, silver, and precious stones, feathers, cloaks, and embroidered goods, and male and female slaves who are also sold there. They bring as many slaves to be sold in that market as the Portuguese bring Negroes from Guinea. Some are brought there attached to long poles by means of collars round their necks to prevent them from escaping, but others are left loose. Next there were those who sold coarser cloth, and cotton goods and fabrics made of twisted thread, and there were chocolate merchants with their chocolate. In this way you could see every kind of merchandise to be found anywhere in New Spain, laid out in the same way as goods are laid out in my own district of Medina del Campo, a centre for fairs, where each line of stalls has its own particular sort. So it was in this great market. There were those who sold sisal cloth and ropes and the sandals they wear on their feet, which are made from the same plant. All these were kept in one part of the market, in the place assigned to them, and in another part were skins of tigers and lions, otters, jackals, and deer, badgers, mountain cats, and other wild animals, some tanned and some untanned, and other classes of merchandise.

. . .

Then there were the sellers of pitch-pine for torches, and other things of that kind, and I must also mention, with all apologies, that they sold many canoe-loads of human excrement, which they keep in the creeks near the market. This was for the manufacture of salt and the curing of skins, which they say cannot be done without it. I know that many gentlemen will laugh at this, but I assure them it is true. I may add that on all the roads they have shelters made of reeds or straw or grass so that they can retire when they wish to do so, and purge their bowels unseen by passers-by, and also in order that their excrement shall not be lost.

But why waste so many words on the goods in their great market? If I describe everything in detail I shall never be done. Paper, which in Mexico they call *amal*, and some reeds that smell of liquidamber, and are full of tobacco, and yellow ointments and other such things, are sold in a separate part. Much cochineal is for sale too, under the arcades of that market, and there are many sellers of herbs and other such things. They have a building there also in which three judges sit, and there are officials like constables who examine the merchandise. I am forgetting the sellers of salt and the makers of flint knives, and how they split them off the stone itself, and the fisherwomen and the men who sell small cakes made from a sort of weed which they get out of the great lake, which curdles and forms a kind of bread which tastes rather like cheese. They sell axes too, made of bronze and copper and tin, and gourds and brightly painted wooden jars.

We went on to the great ***cue***, and as we approached its wide courts, before leaving the market-place itself, we saw many more merchants who, so I was told, brought gold to sell in grains, just as they extract it

Caciques: Nobles.

Cue: Temple.

from the mines. This gold is placed in the thin quills of the large geese of that country, which are so white as to be transparent. They used to reckon their accounts with one another by the length and thickness of these little quills, how much so many cloaks or so many gourds of chocolate or so many slaves were worth, or anything else they were bartering.

WORKING WITH SOURCES

1. How and why does Díaz use comparisons from other markets while describing the one in Tlatelolco?
2. What do the specific elements of this market suggest about the importance of trade and commerce in pre-Columbian Mexico?

15.4 Pedro Cieza de León on Incan Roads, 1541–1547

The Incas created an imperial communications and logistics infrastructure that was unparalleled in the Americas, with two highways extending to the north and south from Cuzco nearly the entire length of the empire. The roads, which were up to 12 feet wide, crossed the terrain as directly as possible, which clearly required a tremendous labor force to create. In many places, even today, the 25,000-mile road network still exists. Pedro Cieza de León was born in Spain in 1520 and undoubtedly traveled along the extensive, and still-functional, Roman road system of his native land as a child. When he arrived in the New World at the age of 13, he was captivated and impressed by the civilizations that the Spanish were supplanting. In 1541, he began writing his account of the Incas, tracing their heritage and government for the benefit of those who would never see the territory he did—or travel the roads that made his observations possible.

CHAPTER 42 (II.XV)

Of how the buildings for the Lord-Incas were constructed, and the highways to travel through the kingdom [of Peru].

One of the things that most took my attention when I was observing and setting down the things of this kingdom was how and in what way the great, splendid highways we see throughout it could be built, and the number of men that must have been required, and what tools and instruments they used to level the mountains and cut through the rock to make them as broad and good as they are. For it seems to me that if the Emperor were to desire another highway built like the one from Quito to Cuzco, or that which goes from Cuzco to Chile, truly I do not believe he could do it, with all his power and the men at his disposal, unless he followed the method the Incas employed. For if it were a question of a road fifty leagues long, or a hundred, or two hundred, we can assume that, however rough the land, it would not be too difficult, working hard, to do it. But there were so long, one of them more than 1100 leagues, over mountains so rough and dismaying that in certain places one could not see bottom, and some of the sierras so sheer and barren that the road had to be cut through the living

---

Source: Pedro Cieza de León, *The Incas*, trans. Harriet de Onis, ed. Victor Wolfgang von Hagen (Norman: University of Oklahoma Press, 1959), 135–137.

rock to keep it level and the right width. All this they did with fire and picks.

. . .

When a Lord-Inca had decided on the building of one of these famous highways, no great provisioning or levies or anything else was needed except for the Lord-Inca to say, let this be done. The inspectors then went through the provinces, laying out the route and assigning Indians from one end to the other to the building of the road. In this way, from one boundary of the province to the other, at its expense and with its Indians, it was built as laid out, in a short time; and the others did the same, and, if necessary, a great stretch of the road was built at the same time, or all of it. When they came to the barren places, the Indians of the lands nearest by came with victuals and tools to do the work, and all was done with little effort and joyfully, because they were not oppressed in any way, nor did the Incas put overseers to watch them.

Aside from these, great fine highways were built, like that which runs through the valley of Xaquixahuana, and comes out of the city of Cuzco and goes by the town of Muhina. There were many of these highways all over the kingdom, both in the highlands and the plains. Of all, four are considered the main highways, and they are those which start from the city of Cuzco, at the square, like a crossroads, and go to the different provinces of the kingdom. As these monarchs held such a high opinion of themselves, when they set out on one of these roads, the royal person with the necessary guard took one [road], and the rest of the people another. So great was their pride that when one of them died, his heir, if he had to travel to a distant place, built his road larger and broader than that of his predecessor, but this was only if this Lord-Inca set out on some conquest, or [performed] some act so noteworthy that it could be said the road built for him was longer.

WORKING WITH SOURCES

1. How were the Incas' roads a manifestation of royal power, at least in Cieza de León's estimation?
2. What technical challenges faced the Incan road builders, and how did they overcome them?

15.5 Garcilaso de la Vega, "The Walls and Gates of Cuzco," 1609–1616

The Incan city of Cuzco was an elongated triangle formed by the confluence of two rivers. At one end, enormous, zigzagging walls followed the contours of a steep hill. The walls were built with stone blocks weighing up to 100 tons and cut so precisely that no mortar was needed. The ruins of the walls were still visible after the Spanish siege of 1536 (as they are today), and they were a marvel to Garcilaso de la Vega, when he viewed them in the mid-sixteenth century. Garcilaso was born in 1539, the decade of the conquest of Peru, to a Spanish conqueror and a Native American princess, a second cousin of the last two Inca rulers. As a young man, Garcilaso left his native Peru never to return. Toward the end of his life he retired to a secluded Spanish village, where he wrote his general history of the Incas. He was particularly proud of the monumental achievements of his Incan relatives, and of the power that their construction projects represented.

Source: Garcilaso de la Vega, *Royal Commentaries of the Incas and General History of Peru*, trans. Harold V. Livermore (Austin: University of Texas Press, 1966), vol. 1, 463–468.

CHAPTER XXVII

The fortress of Cuzco; the size of its stones.

The Inca kings of Peru made marvelous buildings, fortresses, temples, royal palaces, gardens, storehouses, roads, and other constructions of great excellence, as can be seen even today from their remaining ruins, though the whole building can scarcely be judged from the mere foundations.

The greatest and most splendid building erected to show the power and majesty of the Incas was the fortress of Cuzco, the grandeur of which would be incredible to anyone who had not seen it, and even those who have seen it and considered it with attention imagine, and even believe, that it was made by enchantment, the handiwork of demons, rather than of men. Indeed the multiplicity of stones, large and small, of which the three **circumvallations** are composed (and they are more like rocks than stones) makes one wonder how they could have been quarried, for the Indians had neither iron nor steel to work them with. And the question of how they were conveyed to the site is no less difficult a problem, since they had no oxen and could not make wagons: nor would oxen and wagons have sufficed to carry them. They were in fact heaved by main force with the aid of thick cables. The roads by which they were brought were not flat, but rough mountainsides with steep slopes, up and down which the rocks were dragged by human effort alone.

. . .

CHAPTER XXVIII

The three circumvallations, the most remarkable part of the work.

On the other side, opposite this wall, there is a large level space. From this direction the ascent to the top of the hill is a gradual one up which an enemy could advance in order of battle. The Incas therefore made three concentric walls on the slopes, each of which would be more than two hundred fathoms long. They are in the shape of a half moon, for they close together at the ends to meet the other wall of smooth masonry on the side facing the city. The first of these three walls best exhibits the might of the Incas, for although all three are of the same workmanship, it is the most impressive and has the largest stones, making the whole construction seem incredible to anyone who has not seen it, and giving an impression of awe to the careful observer who ponders on the size and number of the stones and the limited resources of the natives for cutting and working them and setting them in their places.

. . .

Almost in the middle of each wall there was a gate, and these gates were each shut with a stone as high and as thick as the wall itself which could be raised and lowered. The first of these was called Tiupuncu, "gate of sand," since the plain is rather sandy or gravelly at this point: *tiu* is "sand," or "a sandy place," and *puncu*, "gate, door." The second is called Acahuana Puncu, after the master mason, whose name was Acahuana, the syllable *ca* being pronounced deep down in the throat. The third is Viracocha Puncu, dedicated to the god Viracocha, the phantom we have referred to at length, who appeared to Prince Viracocha Inca and forewarned him of the rising of the Chancas, as a result of which he was regarded at the defender and second founder of Cuzco, and therefore given this gate with the request that he should guard it and defend the fortress as he had guarded the city and the whole empire in the past.

Circumvallations: Walls built around the city.

WORKING WITH SOURCES

1. Why did the Incas feel the need to fortify Cuzco so heavily, and would these preparations have been successful in typical battle situations?
2. What aspect of the city's walls most arouses Garcilaso's admiration and wonder, and why?

16. THE WESTERN EUROPEAN OVERSEAS EXPANSION AND OTTOMAN-HABSBURG STRUGGLE, 1450–1650

16.1 Christopher Columbus, *The Book of Prophecies*, 1501–1502

Although he is more famous for his voyages—and for the richly detailed accounts he made of them—Columbus (1451–1506) also composed a book of prophetic revelations toward the end of his life, entitled *El Libro de las Profecias*. Written after his third voyage to the Americas, the book traced the development of God's plans for the end of the world, which could be hastened along, particularly by a swift and decisive move to reclaim Jerusalem from Muslim control. When Jerusalem was once more restored to Christian sovereignty, Columbus predicted, Jesus could return to earth, and all of the events foreseen in the Book of Revelation (and in various medieval revelations, as well) could unfold. It is helpful to place the plans for Columbus's original voyage in 1492 against the backdrop of his religious beliefs, as he encourages Ferdinand and Isabella to take their rightful place in God's mystical plan—as well as in Columbus's own cartographic charts.

Letter from the Admiral to the King and Queen [Ferdinand and Isabella]

. . .

Most exalted rulers: At a very early age I began sailing the sea and have continued until now. This profession creates a curiosity about the secrets of the world. I have been a sailor for forty years, and I have personally sailed to all the known regions. I have had commerce and conversation with knowledgeable people of the clergy and the laity. Latins and Greeks, Jews and Moors, and with many others of different religions. Our Lord has favored my occupation and has given me an intelligent mind. He has endowed me with a great talent for seamanship; sufficient ability in astrology, geometry, and arithmetic; and the mental and physical dexterity required to draw spherical maps of cities, rivers and mountains, islands and ports, with everything in its proper place.

During this time I have studied all kinds of texts: cosmography, histories, chronicles, philosophy, and other disciplines. Through these writings, the hand of Our Lord opened my mind to the possibility of sailing to the Indies and gave me the will to attempt the voyage. With this burning ambition I came to your Highnesses. Everyone who heard about my enterprise rejected it with laughter and ridicule. Neither all the sciences that I mentioned previously nor citations drawn from them were of any help to me. Only Your Highnesses had faith and perseverance. Who could doubt that this flash of understanding was the work of the Holy Spirit, as well as my own? The Holy Spirit illuminated his holy and sacred Scripture, encouraging me in a very strong and clear voice from the forty-four books of the Old Testament, the four evangelists, and twenty-three epistles from the blessed apostles, urging me to proceed. Continually, without

Source: Christopher Columbus, *The Book of Prophecies*, ed. Roberto Rusconi, trans. Blair Sullivan (Berkeley: University of California Press, 1997), vol. 3, 67–69, 75–77.

ceasing a moment, they insisted that I go on. Our Lord wished to make something clearly miraculous of this voyage to the Indies in order to encourage me and others about the holy temple.

. . .

Most of the prophecies of holy Scripture have already been fulfilled. The Scriptures say this and the Holy Church loudly and unceasingly is saying it, and no other witness is necessary. I will, however, speak of one prophecy in particular because it bears on my argument and gives me support and happiness whenever I think about it.

I have greatly sinned. Yet, every time that I have asked, I have been covered by the mercy and compassion of Our Lord. I have found the sweetest consolation in throwing off all my cares in order to contemplate his marvelous presence.

I have already said that for the voyage to the Indies neither intelligence nor mathematics nor world maps were of any use to me; it was the fulfillment of Isaiah's prophecy. This is what I want to record here in order to remind Your Highnesses and so that you can take pleasure from the things I am going to tell you about Jerusalem on the basis of the same authority. If you have faith in this enterprise, you will certainly have the victory.

. . .

I said above that much that has been prophesied remains to be fulfilled, and I say that these are the world's great events, and I say that a sign of this is the acceleration of Our Lord's activities in this world. I know this from the recent preaching of the gospel in so many lands.

The Calabrian abbot Joachim said that whoever was to rebuild the temple on Mount Zion would come from Spain.

The cardinal Pierre d'Ailly wrote at length about the end of the religion of Mohammed and the coming of the Antichrist in his treatise *De concordia astronomicae veritatis et narrationis historicae* [*On the agreement between astronomical truth and historical narrative*]; he discusses, particularly in the last nine chapters, what many astronomers have said about the ten revolutions of Saturn.

WORKING WITH SOURCES

1. How does Columbus appeal to the "crusading" goals of Ferdinand and Isabella, and why?
2. Would this appeal have found favor with the monarchs, given their other actions in Spain in 1492?

16.2 Thomas the Eparch and Joshua Diplovatatzes, "The Fall of Constantinople," 1453

The siege and conquest of Constantinople by the Ottoman Turks under Mehmet II (r. 1451–1481) was one of the turning points of world history. Unfolding over two months between April 5 and May 29, 1453, the siege exposed the inability of the Byzantine emperor Constantine XI to withstand a sustained and massive attack. Outnumbering the defenders 11 to 1, the Ottomans battered Constantinople's walls with heavy cannons and took advantage of the natural weaknesses of the

---

Source: trans. William L. North from the Italian version in A. Pertusi, ed., *La Caduta di Constantinopoli: Le testimonianze dei contemporanei* (Milan: Mondadori, 1976), 234–239, available online at https://apps.carleton.edu/curricular/mars/assets/Thomas_the_Eparch_and_Joshua_Diplovatatzes_for_MARS_website.pdf.

city's geography. This account, told by two survivors and (self-proclaimed) eyewitnesses to the siege and its aftermath, details some of the specific stages of the defeat—and the suffering for Christians that came as a result.

When the Turk then drew near to Pera in the fortified zone, he seized all the boats he could find and bound them to each other so as to form a bridge which permitted the combatants to fight on the water just as they did on land. The Turks had with them thousands of ladders which they placed against the walls, right at the place which they had fired [their cannon] and breached the wall, just as they did at the cemetery of St. Sebold. The Genoese handled this breach; they wanted to protect it with their ships because they had so many. In the army of the Turk the order had been given fifteen days before the attack that each soldier would carry a ladder, whether he was fighting on land or sea. There also arrived galleys full of armed men: it seemed that they were Genoese and that they had come to aid the besieged, but in fact they were Turks and they were slipping into the gates. Just as this was becoming less worrisome and the city seemed secure, there arrived under the flag of the Genoese several ships which repelled the Turks with great losses.

At dawn on Monday, 29 May, they began an attack that lasted all night until Tuesday evening and they conquered the city. The commander of the Genoese, who was leading the defense of the breach, pretended to be wounded and abandoned his battle station, taking with him all his people. When the Turks realized this, they slipped in through the breach. When the emperor of the Greeks saw this, he exclaimed in a loud voice: "My God, I have been betrayed!" and he suddenly appeared with his people, exhorting the others to stand firm and defend themselves. But then the gate was opened and the crush of people became such that the emperor himself and his [men] were killed by the Turks and the traitors.

Then the Turks ran to the Hagia Sophia, and all those whom they had imprisoned there, they killed in the first heat of rage. Those whom they found later, they bound with a cord around their neck and their hands tied behind their backs and led them out of the city. When the Turk learned that the emperor had been killed in Constantinople, he captured the Grand Duke who was governing in the emperor's stead and had the Grand Duke's son beheaded and then the Grand Duke himself. Then he seized one of the Grand Duke's daughters who was quite beautiful and made her lie on the great altar of Hagia Sophia with a crucifix under her head and then raped her. Then the most brutish of the Turks seized the finest noble women, virgins, and nuns of the city and violated them in the presence of the Greeks and in sacrilege of Christianity. Then they destroyed all the sacred objects and the bodies of the saints and burned everything they found, save for the cross, the nail, and the clothing of Christ: no one knows where these relics ended up, no one has found them. They also wanted to desecrate the image of the Virgin of St. Luke by stabbing six hundred people in front of it, one after another, like madmen. Then they took prisoner those who fell into their hands, tied them with a rope around the neck and calculated the value of each one. Women had to redeem themselves with their own bodies, men by fornicating with their hands or some other means. Whoever was able to pay the assessed amount could remain in his faith and whoever refused had to die. The Turk who had become governor of Constantinople, named Suleiman in German, occupied the temple of Hagia Sophia to practice his faith there. For three days the Turks sacked and pillaged the city, and each kept whatever he found—people and goods—and did with them whatever he wished.

. . .

All this was made known by Thomas the Eparch, a count of Constantinople, and Joshua Diplovatatzes. Thutros of Constantinople translated their Greek into "welisch" and Dumita Exswinnilwacz and Matheus Hack of Utrecht translated their welisch into German.

WORKING WITH SOURCES

1. What does this account suggest about the preparedness of the Turks for the sack of Constantinople—and the lack of preparation on the part of the Byzantine defenders?
2. What details indicate that the taking of Constantinople was seen as a "religious" war on the Ottoman side?

16.3 Evliya Çelebi, "A Procession of Artisans at Istanbul," ca. 1638

Born on the Golden Horn and raised in the Sultan's palace in Istanbul, Çelebi traveled throughout Ottoman domains between 1640 and 1680. He published an account of his travels and experiences as the *Seyahatname*, or *Book of Travels*. In the first of his ten books in the document, Çelebi provides a lengthy description of Istanbul around the year 1638, including a panoramic view of 1,100 artisan and craft guilds. The numbers and diversity of trades represented underscore the extent of Ottoman commerce—as well as the pride of place each of the city's working people claimed as their due.

The numbers in brackets refer to the order of listing in this chapter.

I: ***Ship-captains [7] vs. Saddlers [30]***
Following the bakers [6], the saddlers wished to pass, but the ship-captains and sea-merchants raised a great fuss. When Sultan Murad got wind of the matter, he consulted with the ulema and the guild shaikhs. They all agreed that it made sense for the ship-captains to proceed after the bakers, because it was they who transported the wheat, and the bakers were dependent on them, and also because Noah was their patron saint.

Comment: the saddlers do not reappear until much later, between the tanners [29] and the shoemakers [31].

. . .

III: ***Egyptian Merchants [9] vs. Butchers [10]***
Following the procession of these Mediterranean Sea captains, the butchers were supposed to pass, according to imperial decree. But all the great Egyptian merchants, including the dealers in rice, hemp, Egyptian reed mats, coffee and sugar gathered together and began quarreling with the butchers. Finally they went before the sultan and said: "My padishah, our galleons are charged with transporting rice, lentils, coffee and hemp. They cannot do without us, nor we without them. Why should these bloody and tricky butchers come between us? Plagues have arisen from cities where they shed their blood, and for fear of this their stalls and shambles in other countries are outside of the city walls. They are a bloody and filthy band of ill-omen. We, on the other hand, always make Istanbul plentiful and cheap with grains of all sorts."

Now the butchers' eyes went bloodshot. "My padishah," they said, "Our patron saint is Butcher Cömerd and our occupation is with sheep, an animal which the Creator has made the object of mercy, and whose flesh He has made lawful food for the strengthening of His servants' bodies. Bread and meat are mentioned as the foremost of God's gifts to mankind: with a small portion of meat, a poor man can subsist for five or six days. We make our living with such a lawful trade, and are known for our generosity (*cömerdlik*). It is we who make Istanbul plentiful and

---

Source: Robert Dankoff, *An Ottoman Mentality: The World of Evliya Çelebi*, 2nd ed. (Leiden, the Netherlands: Brill, 2006), 86–89.

cheap. As for these merchants and dealers and profiteers: concerning them the Koran says (2:275), 'God has made selling lawful and profiteering unlawful'. They are such a despised group that after bringing their goods from Egypt they store it in magazines in order to create a shortage, thus causing public harm through their hoarding.

. . .

"Egyptian sugar? But in the Koran the rivers of paradise are praised as being made 'of pure honey' (47:15). Now we have honey from Turkey, Athens, Wallachia, Moldavia, each with seventy distinct qualities. Furthermore, if my padishah wished, thousands of quintals of sugar could be produced in Alanya, Antalya, Silifke, Tarsus, Adana, Payas, Antakya, Aleppo, Damascus, Sidon, Beyrut, Tripoli and other such provinces—enough to make it plentiful and cheap throughout the world—so why do we need your sugar?

"As for coffee: it is an innovation; it prevents sleep; it dulls the generative powers; and coffee houses are dens of sedition. When roasted it is burnt; and in the legal compilations known as *Bezzaziye* and *Tatarhaniye* we have the dictum that 'Whatever is carbonized is absolutely forbidden'—this holds even for burnt bread. Spiced sherbet, pure milk, tea, fennel, salep, and almond-cream—all these are more wholesome than coffee."

. . .

To these objections of the butchers, the Egyptian merchants replied:

. . . "It is true that Turkey has no need of sugar and hemp, and that European sugar is also very fine. But tell us this, O band of butchers: what benefit and return do you offer to the public treasury?"

The butchers had nothing to say to this, and the Egyptian merchants continued: "My padishah, the goods arriving in our galleons provide the public treasury an annual revenue of 11,000 purses from customs dues. As a matter of justice (*'adalet ederseñiz*) we ought to have precedence in the Muhammadan procession, and the butchers ought to come after us." The *şeyhülislam* Yahya Efendi and Mu'id Ahmed Efendi cited the hadith, "The best of men is he who is useful to mankind," and the sultan gave the Egyptian merchants a noble rescript authorizing them to go first, and the butchers to go second.

WORKING WITH SOURCES

1. Why did the order in which they appeared in the procession matter so much to these particular groups?
2. How did appeals to the Quran accentuate or diminish their case to be placed ahead in the procession?

16.4 Ogier Ghiselin de Busbecq, "The Court of Suleiman the Magnificent," 1581

Ghiselin (1522–1592) was a Flemish ambassador who represented the Austrian Habsburgs at the court of Suleiman the Magnificent (1520–1566) in Istanbul. In 1581, he published an account of his time among the Ottomans as *Itinera Constantinopolitanum et Amasianum* (*Travels in Constantinople and Asia Minor*). In this segment of his travel narrative, he draws attention to the personal habits

Source: Wayne S. Vucinich, *The Ottoman Empire: Its Record and Legacy* (Princeton, NJ: Van Nostrand, 1965), 127–129.

and behaviors of a contemporary emperor—one who saw himself as the heir to the Romans as well as to the other monarchs who had held Constantinople/Istanbul.

The Sultan was seated on a very low ottoman, not more than a foot from the ground, which was covered with a quantity of costly rugs and cushions of exquisite workmanship; near him lay his bow and arrows. His air, as I said, was by no means gracious, and his face wore a stern, though dignified, expression. On entering we were separately conducted into the royal presence by the chamberlains, who grasped our arms. . . . After having gone through a pretense of kissing his hand, we were conducted backwards to the wall opposite his seat, care being taken that we should never turn our backs on him. The Sultan then listened to what I had to say; but the language I held was not at all to his taste, for the demands of his Majesty breathed a spirit of independence and dignity . . . and so he made no answer beyond saying in a tetchy way, "Giusel, giusel," i.e. well, well . . .

. . .

I was greatly struck with the silence and order that prevailed in this great crowd. There were no cries, no hum of voices, the usual accompaniments of a motley gathering, neither was there any jostling; without the slightest disturbance each man took his proper place according to his rank. The Agas, as they call their chiefs, were seated, to wit, generals, colonels (*bimbashi*), and captains (*soubashi*). Men of a lower position stood. The most interesting sight in this assembly was a body of several thousand Janissaries, who were drawn up in a long line apart from the rest; their array was so steady and motionless that, being at a little distance, it was some time before I could make up my mind as to whether they were human beings or statues; at last I received a hint to salute them, and saw all their heads bending at the same moment to return my bow.

. . .

When the cavalry had ridden past, they were followed by a long procession of Janissaries, but few of whom carried any arms except their regular weapon, the musket. They were dressed in uniforms of almost the same shape and colour, so that you might recognize them to be the slaves. . . . There is only one thing in which they are extravagant, viz., plumes, headdresses, etc., and veterans who formed the rear guard were specially distinguished by ornaments of this kind. The plumes which they insert in their frontlets might well be mistaken for a walking forest.

WORKING WITH SOURCES

1. Why were order and discipline apparently so important at Suleiman's court?
2. Why might Ghiselin have found the Janissaries so particularly impressive?

16.5 Janissary Musket, ca. 1750–1800

The Janissaries constitute the most famous and centralized of the Ottomans' military institutions. A feared and respected military fource, the Janissaries were Christian-born males who had been seized from their homes as boys, converted to Islam, and then trained as future soldiers and administrators for the Turks. Under the direct orders of the sultan and his viziers, the Janissaries were equipped with the latest military innovations. In the early fifteenth century, these units received cannons and matchlock muskets. The muskets continued their evolution in the Janissaries' hands, becoming the standard equipment for Ottoman and other armies.

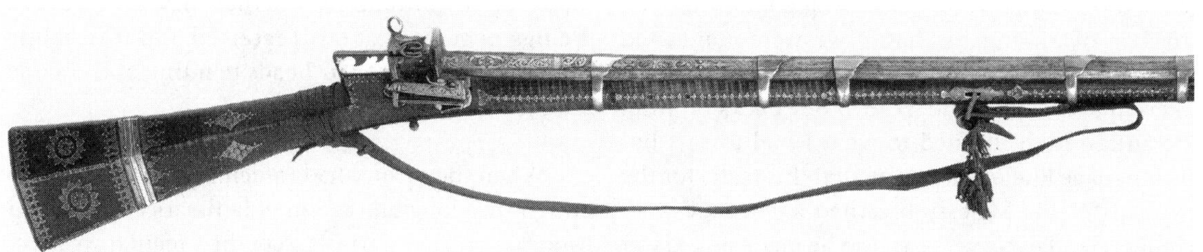

WORKING WITH SOURCES

1. What does the elaborate decoration of the musket suggest about its psychological, as well as its practical, effects?
2. Was this firearm likely to have been produced by indigenous, rather than European, gunsmiths? Why or why not?

17. THE RENAISSANCE, NEW SCIENCES, AND RELIGIOUS WARS IN EUROPE, 1450–1750

17.1 Examination of Lady Jane Grey, London, 1554

Jane Grey, the granddaughter of Henry VIII's sister Mary, was born in 1537, the same year as Edward VI, the only surviving son of the king who had sought a male heir so desperately. Jane, who like Edward was raised in the Protestant religion Henry had introduced to England, proved a diligent and intellectually gifted teenager. In spite of her youth and gender, Jane corresponded with Protestant authorities on the Continent, but fast-moving events in England precluded further study. When Edward died without an heir in 1553, the throne passed, by prearranged agreement, to his fiercely Catholic half-sister Mary.

However, in order to forestall a Catholic successor—and the dramatic rollback of the Protestant reforms instituted by Henry's and Edward's Church of England—Jane's relatives proclaimed her queen. Her rule lasted a mere nine days. She was imprisoned in the Tower of London by Mary, who was then forced to consider whether Jane's execution was warranted. Shortly before Jane's death, at age 16, Queen Mary sent her own chaplain, Master Feckenham (sometimes rendered as "Fecknam") to try to reconcile Jane to the Catholic faith. The results of this attempt were triumphantly recorded in John Foxe's *Acts and Monuments*, published after the Protestant Queen Elizabeth had triumphed over Mary and the Catholics. Although the conversation recorded here is not a trial transcript—and is a highly partisan account—it does distill some of the central issues that divided Catholics and Protestants in an extremely chaotic and violent period.

FECKNAM: "I am here come to you at this present, sent from the queen [Mary] and her council, to instruct you in the true doctrine of the right faith: although I have so great confidence in you, that I shall have, I trust, little need to travail with you much therein."

JANE: "Forsooth, I heartily thank the queen's highness, which is not unmindful of her humble subject: and I hope, likewise, that you no less will do your duty therein both truly and faithfully, according to that you were sent for."

. . .

FECKNAM: "How many sacraments are there?"

JANE: "Two: the one the sacrament of baptism, and the other the sacrament of the Lord's Supper."

FECKNAM: "No, there are seven."

JANE: "By what Scripture find you that?"

FECKNAM: "Well, we will talk of that hereafter. But what is signified by your two sacraments?"

JANE: "By the sacrament of baptism I am washed with water and regenerated by the Spirit, and that washing is a token to me that I am the child of God. The sacrament of the Lord's

Source: "The Examination of Lady Jane Grey (1554)," from Denis R. Janz, ed., *A Reformation Reader: Primary Texts with Introductions*, 2nd ed. (Minneapolis, MN: Fortress, 2008), 360–362, taken from *The Acts and Monuments of John Foxe* (London: Seeleys, 1859), 415–417.

Supper, offered unto me, is a sure seal and testimony that I am, by the blood of Christ, which he shed for me on the cross, made partaker of the everlasting kingdom."

FECKNAM: "Why? What do you receive in that sacrament? Do you not receive the very body and blood of Christ?"

JANE: "No, surely, I do not so believe. I think that at the supper I neither receive flesh nor blood, but bread and wine: which bread when it is broken, and the wine when it is drunken, put me in remembrance how that for my sins the body of Christ was broken, and his blood shed on the cross; and with that bread and wine I receive the benefits that come by the breaking of his body, and shedding of his blood, for our sins on the cross."

FECKNAM: "Why, doth not Christ speak these words, 'Take, eat, this is my body?' Require you any plainer words? Doth he not say, it is his body?"

JANE: "I grant, he saith so; and so he saith, 'I am the vine, I am the door'; but he is never the more for that, the door or the vine. Doth not St. Paul say, 'He calleth things that are not, as though they were?' God forbid that I should say, that I eat the very natural body and blood of Christ: for then either I should pluck away my redemption, or else there were two bodies, or two Christs. One body was tormented on the cross, and if they did eat another body, then had he two bodies: or if his body were eaten, then was it not broken upon the cross; or if it were broken upon the cross, it was not eaten of his disciples."

. . .

With these and like such persuasions he would have had her lean to the [Catholic] church, but it would not be. There were many more things whereof they reasoned, but these were the chiefest.

After this, Fecknam took his leave, saying, that he was sorry for her: "For I am sure," quoth he, "that we two shall never meet."

JANE: "True it is," said she, "that we shall never meet, except God turn your heart; for I am assured, unless you repent and turn to God, you are in an evil case. And I pray God, in the bowels of his mercy, to send you his Holy Spirit; for he hath given you his great gift of utterance, if it please him also to open the eyes of your heart."

WORKING WITH SOURCES

1. What does this source reveal about the religious education of young people in the extended royal household during the final years of Henry VIII and the reign of Edward VI?
2. How does the literal interpretation of the Bible enter into this discussion, and why?

17.2 Sebastian Castellio, *Concerning Whether Heretics Should Be Persecuted*, 1554

In October 1553, the extraordinarily gifted Spanish scientist Michael Servetus was executed with the approval and the strong support of John Calvin and his followers in Geneva. The charge was heresy, specifically for denying the existence of the Trinity and the divinity of Christ, and the method of execution—burning at the stake—elicited commentary and protest from across

---

Source: Sebastian Castellio, *Concerning Heretics, Whether They Are to Be Persecuted and How They Are to Be Treated, A Collection of the Opinions of Learned Men Both Ancient and Modern*, trans. Roland H. Bainton (New York: Octagon, 1965), 132–134.

Europe. One of the fullest and most sophisticated protests against this execution was issued by Sebastian Castellio, a professor of Greek language and New Testament theology in the Swiss city of Basel. His book *De Haereticis* is a collection of opinions, drawn from Christian writers, from both before and after the Protestant Reformation and across 15 centuries. It is more than an academic exercise, however, as this dedication of the Latin work to a German noble demonstrates.

From the Dedication of the book to Duke Christoph of Württemberg:

. . . And just as the **Turks** disagree with the Christians as to the person of Christ, and the Jews with both the Turks and the Christians, and the one condemns the other and holds him for a heretic, so Christians disagree with Christians on many points with regard to the teaching of Christ, and condemn one another and hold each other for heretics. Great controversies and debates occur as to baptism, the Lord's Supper, the invocation of the saints, justification, free will, and other obscure questions, so that Catholics, Lutherans, Zwinglians, Anabaptists, monks, and others condemn and persecute one another more cruelly than the Turks do the Christians. These dissensions arise solely from ignorance of the truth, for if these matters were so obvious and evident as that there is but one God, all Christians would agree among themselves on these points as readily as all nations confess that God is one.

What, then is to be done in such great contentions? We should follow the counsel of Paul, "Let not him that eateth despise him that eateth not. . . . To his own master he standeth or falleth." [Romans 14:3–4] Let not the Jews or Turks condemn the Christians, nor let the Christians condemn the Jews or Turks, but rather teach and win them by true religion and justice, and let us, who are Christians, not condemn one another, but, if we are wiser than they, let us also be better and more merciful. This is certain that the better a man knows the truth, the less is he inclined to condemn, as appears in the case of Christ and the apostles. But he who lightly condemns others shows thereby that he knows nothing precisely, because he cannot bear others, for to know is to know how to put into practice. He who does not know how to act mercifully and kindly does not know the nature of mercy and kindness, just as he who cannot blush does not know the nature of shame.

If we were to conduct ourselves in this fashion we should be able to dwell together in concord. Even though in some matters we disagreed, yet should we consent together and forbear one another in love, which is the bond of peace, until we arrive at the unity of the faith [Ephesians 4:2–3]. But now, when we strive with hate and persecutions we go from bad to worse. Nor are we mindful of our office, since we are wholly taken up with condemnation, and the Gospel because of us is made a reproach unto the heathen [Ezekiel 22:4], for when they see us attacking one another with the fury of beasts, and the weak oppressed by the strong, these heathen feel horror and detestation for the Gospel, as if it made men such, and they abominate even Christ himself, as if he commanded men to do such things. We rather degenerate into Turks and Jews than convert them into Christians. Who would wish to be a Christian, when he saw that those who confessed the name of Christ were destroyed by Christians themselves with fire, water, and the sword without mercy and more cruelly treated than brigands and murderers? Who would not think Christ a **Moloch**, or some such god, if he wished that men should be immolated to him and burned alive? Who would wish to serve Christ on condition that a difference of opinion on a controversial point with those in authority would be punished by burning alive at the command of Christ himself more cruelly than in the bull of **Phalaris**, even

---

Turks: Muslims.

Moloch: A Phoenician deity who, according to the Bible, demanded the sacrifice of human children.

Phalaris: Tyrant in pre-Christian Sicily who burned victims alive in a giant bronze bull.

though from the midst of the flames he should call with a loud voice upon Christ, and should cry out that he believed in Him? Imagine Christ, the judge of all, present. Imagine Him pronouncing the sentence and applying the torch. Who would not hold Christ for a Satan? What more could Satan do than burn those who call upon the name of Christ?

WORKING WITH SOURCES

1. Was Castellio minimizing the significant theological disputes that had arisen as a result of the Reformation? Were his objections directly applicable to the Servetus case?
2. What did Castellio see as the practical, as well as the theological, consequences of burning those perceived to be "heretics"? Is he convincing on this point?

17.3 Duc de Saint-Simon, "The Daily Habits of Louis XIV at Versailles," ca. 1715

A minor noble at Louis XIV's court at Versailles, Louis de Rouvroy, the duc de Saint-Simon (1675–1755), would achieve lasting fame after his death with the publication of his copious, frank, and witty observations of the court. While resident at Versailles for brief periods after 1702 until the king's death in 1715, Saint-Simon paid particular attention to the maneuverings of his fellow aristocrats. He managed to garner the resentment of many of them, especially the king's illegitimate children, "the Bastards," who held a prominent place at court. His accounts of the daily routine of life at Versailles, and the central position of the king who had famously declared, "L'état, c'est moi!," are often applied today to spectacles that can also be described as at once grand and a little absurd.

At eight o'clock the chief valet de chambre on duty, who alone had slept in the royal chamber, and who had dressed himself, awoke the King. The chief physician, the chief surgeon, and the nurse (as long as she lived), entered at the same time. The latter kissed the King; the others rubbed and often changed his shirt, because he was in the habit of sweating a great deal. At the quarter [hour], the grand chamberlain was called (or, in his absence, the first gentleman of the chamber), and those who had, what was called the *grandes entrées*. The chamberlain (or chief gentleman) drew back the curtains which had been closed again, and presented the holy water from the vase, at the head of the bed. These gentlemen stayed but a moment, and that was the time to speak to the King, if any one had anything to ask of him; in which case the rest stood aside. When, contrary to custom, nobody had aught to say, they were there but for a few moments. He who had opened the curtains and presented the holy water, presented also a prayer-book. Then all passed into the cabinet of the council. A very short religious service being over, the King called, they reentered. The same officer gave him his dressing-gown; immediately after, other privileged courtiers entered, and then everybody, in time to find the King putting on his shoes and stockings, for he did almost everything

Source: Memoirs of the Duc de Saint-Simon, trans. Bayle St. John, ed. W. H. Lewis (New York: Macmillan, 1964), 140–141, 144–145.

himself and with address and grace. Every other day we saw him shave himself; and he had a little short wig in which he always appeared, even in bed, and on medicine days. He often spoke of the chase, and sometimes said a word to somebody. No toilette table was near him; he had simply a mirror held before him.

As soon as he was dressed, he prayed to God, at the side of his bed, where all the clergy present knelt, the cardinals without cushions, all the laity remaining standing; and the captain of the guards came to the balustrade during the prayer, after which the King passed into his cabinet.

He found there, or was followed by all who had the entrée, a very numerous company, for it included everybody in any office. He gave orders to each for the day; thus within half a quarter of an hour it was known what he meant to do; and then all this crowd left directly. The bastards, a few favourites, and the valets alone were left. It was then a good opportunity for talking with the King; for example, about plans of gardens and buildings; and conversation lasted more or less according to the person engaged in it.

. . .

At ten o'clock his supper was served. The captain of the guard announced this to him. A quarter of an hour after the King came to supper, and from the antechamber of Madame de Maintenon [his principal mistress] to the table again, any one spoke to him who wished. This supper was always on a grand scale, the royal household (that is, the sons and daughters of France), at table, and a large number of courtiers and ladies present, sitting or standing, and on the evening before the journey to Marly all those ladies who wished to take part in it. That was called presenting yourself for Marly. Men asked in the morning, simply saying to the King, "Sire, Marly." In later years, the King grew tired of this, and a valet wrote up in the gallery the names of those who asked. The ladies continued to present themselves.

. . .

The King, wishing to retire, went and fed his dogs; then said good night, passed into his chamber to the ***ruelle*** of his bed, where he said his prayers, as in the morning, then undressed. He said good night with an inclination of the head, and whilst everybody was leaving the room stood at the corner of the mantelpiece, where he gave the order to the colonel of the guards alone. Then commenced what was called the *petit coucher*, at which only the specially privileged remained. That was short. They did not leave until he got into bed. It was a moment to speak to him.

Ruelle: The "little path" between a bed and the wall.

WORKING WITH SOURCES

1. Why does Saint-Simon pay particular attention to moments of the day during which a courtier could speak directly with the king?
2. What does the combination of religious and secular pursuits in the king's daily habits suggest about life at his court?

17.4 Giorgio Vasari, *The Life of Michelangelo Buonarroti*, 1550

Trained as a painter, architect, and goldsmith, Giorgio Vasari (1511–1574) practiced various artistic trades, but is most renowned today as the first art historian. His *Lives of the Most Eminent Painters, Sculptors, and Architects*, first published in 1550, is the principal source of information about the most prominent artists of the European Renaissance. Having studied under the great artist

Michelangelo Buonarroti (1475–1564), Vasari was particularly keen to tell this story. In these scenes from his biography of Michelangelo, Vasari draws attention to his master's early training, as well as the prominent roles Lorenzo il Magnifico de' Medici and ancient sculpture played in his artistic development.

In those days Lorenzo de' Medici the Magnificent kept Bertoldo the sculptor in his garden near Piazza San Marco, not so much as the custodian or guardian of the many beautiful antiquities he had collected and assembled there at great expense, but rather because he wished above all else to create a school for excellent painters and sculptors. . . . Thus, Domenico [Ghirlandaio] gave him some of his best young men, including among others Michelangelo and Francesco Granacci; and when they went to the garden, they found that Torrigiani, a young man of the Torrigiani family, was there working on some clay figures in the round that Bertoldo had given him to do.

After Michelangelo saw these figures, he made some himself to rival those of Torrigiani, so that Lorenzo, seeing his high spirit, always had great expectations for him, and, encouraged after only a few days, Michelangelo began copying with a piece of marble the antique head of an old and wrinkled faun with a damaged nose and a laughing mouth, which he found there. Although Michelangelo had never before touched marble or chisels, the imitation turned out so well that Lorenzo was astonished, and when Lorenzo saw that Michelangelo, following his own fantasy rather than the antique head, had carved its mouth open to give it a tongue and to make all its teeth visible, this lord, laughing with pleasure as was his custom, said to him: "But you should have known that old men never have all their teeth and that some of them are always missing." In that simplicity of his, it seemed to Michelangelo, who loved and feared this lord, that Lorenzo was correct; and as soon as Lorenzo left, he immediately broke a tooth on the head and dug out the gum in such a way that it seemed the tooth had fallen out, and anxiously awaited Lorenzo's return, who, after coming back and seeing Michelangelo's simplicity and excellence, laughed about it on more than one occasion, recounting it to his friends as if it were miraculous. . . .

. . .

Around this time it happened that Piero Soderini saw the statue [the *David*, finished in 1504], and it pleased him greatly, but while Michelangelo was giving it the finishing touches, he told Michelangelo that he thought the nose of the figure was too large. Michelangelo, realizing that the Gonfaloniere [a civic official in Florence] was standing under the giant and that his viewpoint did not allow him to see it properly, climbed up the scaffolding to satisfy Soderini (who was behind him nearby), and having quickly grabbed the chisel in his left hand along with a little marble dust that he found on the planks in the scaffolding, Michelangelo began to tap lightly with the chisel, allowing the dust to fall little by little without retouching the nose from the way it was. Then, looking down at the Gonfaloniere who stood there watching, he ordered:

"Look at it now."

"I like it better," replied the Gonfaloniere: "you've made it come alive."

Thus Michelangelo climbed down, and, having contented this lord, he laughed to himself, feeling compassion for those who, in order to make it appear that they understand, do not realize what they are saying; and when the statue was finished and set in its foundation, he uncovered it, and to tell the truth, this work eclipsed all other statues, both modern and ancient, whether Greek or Roman; and it can be said that neither the Marforio in Rome, nor the Tiber and the Nile of the Belvedere, nor the colossal statues of Monte Cavallo can be compared to this David, which Michelangelo completed with so much measure and beauty, and so much skill.

Source: Giorgio Vasari, *The Lives of the Artists* (New York: Oxford University Press, 1998), 418–420; 427–428.

WORKING WITH SOURCES

1. How do these anecdotes illustrate the relationship between artists and their patrons (and funders) during the Renaissance?
2. How did Michelangelo deal with the legacy of artists from Greco-Roman antiquity?

17.5 Galileo Galilei, Letter to the Grand Duchess Christina de' Medici, 1615

This famous letter is often cited as an early sign of Galileo's inevitable conflict with church authorities over the Copernican system of planetary motion—and the theory's theological, as well as its scientific, ramifications. Galileo (1564–1642) would be condemned to house arrest in 1632 and forced to make a public repudiation of the heliocentric theory first advanced by Copernicus in the sixteenth century. However, Galileo's connection to the renowned Medici family of Florence was also cause for comment—and caution—from 1610, when he received an appointment and their implicit endorsement.

Constructing a telescope in 1609 (which he proudly claimed could "magnify objects more than 60 times"), Galileo trained it on the moons of Jupiter, which he tracked over several days in 1610. Having named these objects for the Medici family, he rushed these and many other astronomical observations into print in the *Sidereus Nuncius* (*The Starry Messenger*). Inviting other scientists to "apply themselves to examine and determine" these planetary motions, Galileo demonstrated a preference for the Copernican theory and elicited sharp responses, particularly from church officials. In 1615, the dowager Grand Duchess Christina, mother of his patron, Cosimo II, expressed her own reservations about the implications of the Copernican theory for a passage in the Old Testament. Galileo's response attempts, or seems to attempt, to reconcile experimental science and received religion.

Thus let these people apply themselves to refuting the arguments of Copernicus and of the others, and let them leave its condemnation as erroneous and heretical to the proper authorities; but let them not hope that the very cautious and very wise Fathers and the Infallible One with his absolute wisdom are about to make rash decisions like those into which they would be rushed by their special interests and feelings. For in regard to these and other similar propositions which do not directly involve the faith, no one can doubt that the Supreme Pontiff always has the absolute power of permitting or condemning them; however, no creature has the power of making them be true or false, contrary to what they happen to be by nature and de facto. So it seems more advisable to first become sure about the necessary and immutable truth of the matter, over which no one has control, than to condemn one side when such certainty is lacking; this would imply a loss of freedom of decision and of choice insofar as it would give necessity to things which are presently indifferent, free, and dependent on the will of the supreme authority.

Source: Galileo Galilei, *The Essential Galileo*, ed. and trans. Maurice A. Finocchiaro (Indianapolis: Hackett, 2008), §4.2.5—4.2.6, 140–144.

In short, if it is inconceivable that a proposition should be declared heretical when one thinks that it may be true, it should be futile for someone to try to bring about the condemnation of the earth's motion and sun's rest unless he first shows it to be impossible and false.

There remains one last thing for us to examine: to what extent it is true that the Joshua passage [Joshua 10:12–13] can be taken without altering the literal meaning of the words, and how it can be that, when the sun obeyed Joshua's order to stop, from this it followed that the day was prolonged by a large amount.

. . .

I think therefore, if I am not mistaken, that one can clearly see that, given the Ptolemaic system, it is necessary to interpret the words in a way different from their literal meaning. Guided by St. Augustine's very useful prescriptions, I should say that the best nonliteral interpretation is not necessarily this, if anyone can find another which is perhaps better and more suitable. So now I want to examine whether the same miracle could be understood in a way more in accordance with what we read in Joshua, if to the Copernican system we add another discovery which I recently made about the solar body. However, I continue to speak with the same reservations—to the effect that I am not so enamored with my own opinions as to want to place them ahead of those of others; nor do I believe it is impossible to put forth interpretations which are better and more in accordance with the Holy Writ.

Let us first assume in accordance with the opinion of the above-mentioned authors, that in the Joshua miracle the whole system of heavenly motions was stopped, so that the stopping of only one would not introduce unnecessarily universal confusion and great turmoil in the whole order of nature.

. . .

Furthermore, what deserves special appreciation, if I am not mistaken, is that with the Copernican system one can very clearly and very easily give a literal meaning to another detail which one reads about the same miracle; that is, that the sun stopped in the middle of heaven. Serious theologians have raised a difficulty about this passage: it seems very probable that, when Joshua asked for the prolongation of the day, the sun was close to setting and not at the meridian; for it was then about the time of the summer solstice, and consequently the days were very long, so that if the sun had been at the meridian then it does not seem likely that it would have been necessary to pray for a lengthening of the day in order to win a battle, since the still remaining time of seven hours or more could very well have been sufficient.

. . .

We can remove this and every other implausibility, if I am not mistaken, by placing the sun, as the Copernican system does and as it is most necessary to do, in the middle, namely, at the center of the heavenly orbs and of the planetary revolutions; for at any hour of the day, whether at noon or in the afternoon, the day would have been lengthened and all heavenly turnings stopped by the sun stopping in the middle of the heavens, namely, at the center of the heavens, where it is located. Furthermore, this interpretation agrees all the more with the literal meaning inasmuch as, if one wanted to claim that the sun's stopping occurred at the noon hour, then the proper expression to use would have been to say that it "stood still at the meridian point," or "at the meridian circle," and not "in the middle of the heaven"; in fact, for a spherical body such as heaven, the middle is really and only the center.

WORKING WITH SOURCES

1. How does Galileo deal with the apparently irreconcilable conclusions of science and the Bible?
2. How would you characterize Galileo's tone in his analysis of the verses from the Book of Joshua?

18. NEW PATTERNS IN NEW WORLDS: COLONIALISM AND INDIGENOUS RESPONSES IN THE AMERICAS, 1500–1800

18.1 Hernán Cortés, *Second Letter from Mexico to Emperor Charles V*, 1522

With a handful of untrained and poorly equipped soldiers, Hernán Cortés overthrew the powerful Aztec civilization between 1519 and 1520. Born in Spain around 1485, Cortés decided to inform the king of Spain (and Holy Roman emperor) Charles V of his achievements, in a series of written updates. Despite their ostensible purpose, these "letters" were designed for more than the edification and delight of the emperor. Like Julius Caesar's dispatches from the Gallic Wars of the 50s BCE—in which at least one million Gauls were killed and another million enslaved—these accounts were designed for broad public consumption. Each letter was sent to Spain as soon as it was ready, and it seems likely that Cortés's father, Martín, arranged for their immediate publication. Over the course of these five published letters, although Cortés developed a persona for himself as a conquering hero and agent of imperial power, he also exposed the ruthlessness and brutality of his "conquest" of Mexico.

From henceforth they offered themselves as vassals of Your Sacred Majesty and swore to remain so always and to serve and assist in all things that Your Highness commanded them. A notary set all this down through the interpreters which I had. Still I determined to go with them; on the one hand, so as not to show weakness and, on the other, because I hoped to conduct my business with Mutezuma from that city because it bordered on his territory, as I have said, and on the road between the two there is free travel and no frontier restrictions.

When the people of Tascalteca saw my determination it distressed them considerably, and they told me many times that I was mistaken, but since they were vassals of Your Sacred Majesty and my friends they would go with me to assist me in whatever might happen. Although I opposed this and asked them not to come, as it was unnecessary, they followed me with some 100,000 men, all well armed for war, and came within two leagues of the city. After much persuasion on my part they returned, though there remained in my company some five or six thousand of them. That night I slept in a ditch, hoping to divest myself of these people in case they caused trouble in the city, and because it was already late enough and I did not want to enter too late. The following morning, they came out of the city to greet me with many trumpets and drums, including many persons whom they regard as priests in their temples, dressed in traditional vestments and singing after their fashion, as they do in the temples. With such ceremony they led us into the city and gave us very good quarters, where all those in my company were most comfortable. There they brought us food, though not sufficient.

. . .

Source: Hernán Cortés: Letters from Mexico, edited and translated by Anthony Pagden (Yale University Press, 1986), 72–74.

During the three days I remained in that city they fed us worse each day, and the lords and principal persons of the city came only rarely to see and speak with me. And being somewhat disturbed by this, my interpreter, who is an Indian woman from Putunchan, which is the great river of which I spoke to Your Majesty in the first letter, was told by another Indian woman and a native of this city that very close by many of Mutezuma's men were gathered, and that the people of the city had sent away their women and children and all their belongings, and were about to fall on us and kill us all; and that if she wished to escape she should go with her and she would shelter her. All this she told to Gerónimo de Aguilar, an interpreter whom I acquired in Yucatán, of whom I have also written to Your Highness; and he informed me. I then seized one of the natives of this city who was passing by and took him aside secretly and questioned him; and he confirmed what the woman and the natives of Tascalteca had told me. Because of this and because of the signs I had observed, I decided to forestall an attack, and I sent for some of the chiefs of the city, saying that I wished to speak with them. I put them in a room and meanwhile warned our men to be prepared, when a harquebus was fired, to fall on the many Indians who were outside our quarters and on those who were inside. And so it was done, that after I had put the chiefs in the room, I left them bound up and rode away and had the harquebus fired, and we fought so hard that in two hours more than three thousand men were killed.

. . .

After fifteen or twenty days which I remained there the city and the land were so pacified and full of people that it seemed as if no one were missing from it, and their markets and trade were carried on as before. I then restored the friendly relations between this city of Curultecal and Tascalteca, which had existed in the recent past, before Mutezuma had attracted them to his friendship with gifts and made them enemies of the others.

WORKING WITH SOURCES

1. Does Cortés offer a justification for his treatment of the people of Tascalteca? Why or why not?
2. What were the risks associated with Cortés's reliance on translators as he conquered the natives of Mexico?

18.2 Marina de San Miguel's Confessions before the Inquisition, Mexico City, 1598–1599

The Inquisition was well established in Spain at the time of Cortés's conquest in the 1520s. A tribunal of the Holy Office of the Inquisition came in the conquistadors' wake, ultimately established at Mexico City in 1571 with authority to regulate Catholic morality throughout "New Spain." Most of the Inquisition trials concerned petty breaches of religious conduct, but others dealt with the much more serious crime of heresy. In November 1598, the Inquisition became alarmed about the rise of a group who believed that the Day of Judgment was at hand. Among the group denounced to the Holy Office was Marina de San Miguel, a Spanish-born woman who held

Source: Jacqueline Holler, "The Spiritual and Physical Ecstasies of a Sixteenth-Century Beata: Marina de San Miguel Confesses Before the Mexican Inquisition," in Richard Boyer and Geoffrey Spurling, eds., *Colonial Lives: Documents on Latin American History, 1550–1850* (New York: Oxford University Press, 2000), 79–98.

a high status due to her mystical visions. Her confessions, offered between November 1598 and January 1599, reveal the degree to which confessions of "deviance" could be extorted from a victim. In March 1601, Marina was stripped naked to the waist and paraded upon a mule. Forced to confess her errors, she was sentenced to 100 lashes with a whip.

First Confession
In the city of Mexico, Friday, November 20, 1598. The Lord Inquisitor *licenciado* don Alonso de Peralta in his morning audience ordered that a woman be brought before him from one of the secret prisons of this Holy Office. Being present, she swore an oath *en forma devida de derecho** under which she promised to tell the truth here in this audience and in all the others that might be held until the determination of her case, and to keep secret everything that she might see or believe or that might be talked about with her or that might happen concerning this her case.

. . .

She was asked if she knows, presumes, or suspects the cause for her arrest and imprisonment in the prisons of the Holy Office. . . . The inquisitor said that with her illness she must have imagined it. And she says that she wants to go over her memory so that she can tell the truth about everything that she might remember.

With this the audience ceased, because it was past eleven. The above was read and she approved it and signed it. And she was ordered to return to her cell, very admonished to examine her memory as she was offered to do.

. . .

Third Confession
In the city of Mexico, Tuesday, November 24, 1598. . . .

She said that what she has remembered is that in the course of her life some spiritual things have happened to her, which she has talked about to some people. And she believes that they have been the cause of her imprisonment, because they were scandalized by what she told them.

. . .

And then she opened her eyes and began to shake and get up from the bench on which she was seated, saying, "My love, help me God, how strongly you have given me this." And among these words she said to the Lord Inquisitor that when she is given these trances, she should be shaken vigorously to awaken her from her deep dream. Then she returned to being as though sleeping. The inquisitor called her by her name and she did not respond, nor the second time. And the third time she opened her eyes and made faces, and made signs with her hands to her mouth.

. . .

Sixth Confession
In the city of Mexico, Monday, January 25, 1599. . . .

She said that it's like this. . . . She has been condemned to hell, because for fifteen years she has had a sensual temptation of the flesh, which makes her perform dishonest acts with her own hands on her shameful parts. She came to pollution [orgasm] saying dishonest words that provoke lust, calling by their dishonest names many dirty and lascivious things. She was tempted to this by the devil, who appeared to her internally in the form of an Angel of Light, who told her that she should do these things, because they were no sin. This was to make her abandon her scruples. And the devil appeared to her in the form of Christ our Redeemer, in such a way that she might uncover her breasts and have carnal union with him. And thus, for fifteen years, she has had carnal union occasionally from month to month, or every two months. And if it had been more she would accuse herself of that too, because she is only trying to save her soul, with no regard to honor or the world. And the carnal act that the devil as Angel of Light and in the form of Christ had with her was the same as if she had had it with a man. And he kissed her, and she enjoyed it, and she felt a great ardor in her whole body, with particular delight and pleasure.

. . .

Eighth Confession
In the city of Mexico, Wednesday, January 27, 1599. . . .

But all the times she had the copulation with the devil in the form of Christ she doubted whether it was the devil or not, from which doubts one can infer that she did not believe as firmly as she ought to have that such things could not possibly be from Christ. In this she should urgently discharge her conscience. . . .

. . .

After the *Ninth Confession*:
In the city of Mexico, Tuesday, Day of the Purification of our Lady, February 2, 1599, the Lord Inquisitor in his afternoon audience ordered Marina de San Miguel brought before him. And once present she was told that if she has remembered anything in her case she should say it, and the truth, under the oath that she has made.

She said no. . . .

WORKING WITH SOURCES

1. What does this document indicate about the working methods of the Inquisition (and their "successes") in Mexico in the 1590s?
2. Does the Inquisition seem to have been more concerned about Marina's sexuality than her mystical "experiences?"

18.3 Nahuatl Land Sale Documents, Mexico, ca. 1610s

After the conquest of the Aztec imperial capital of Tenochtitlan, Spaniards turned their attention to the productive farmland in the surrounding countryside, which was inhabited by Nahuatl-speaking native people. By the late sixteenth century, Spaniards began to expand rapidly into this territory. They acquired estates in a variety of ways, from royal grants to open seizure of property. Nevertheless, the purchase of plots of land from individual Nahuas was also common—although sometimes the sellers came to regret the transaction and petitioned higher authorities for redress of their grievances.

Here in the ***altepetl*** Santo Domingo Mixcoac, Marquesado del Valle, on the first day of July of the year 1612, I, Joaquín de San Francisco, and my wife, Juana Feliciana, citizens here in the ***altepetl*** of Santa María Purificación Tlilhuacan, sell to Dr. Diego de León Plaza, ***teopixqui***, one field and house that we have in the ***tlaxilacalli*** Tlilhuacan next to the house of Juan Bautista, Spaniard. Where we are is right in the middle of [in between] their houses. And now we receive [the money] in person. The reason we sell it is that we have no children to whom it might belong. For there is another land and house, but [the land] here we can no longer [work] because it is really in the middle of [land belonging to] Spaniards. [The land] is not *tributario*, for my father, named Juan Altamirano, and my mother, María Catalina, really left it to me. And now I give it to [the doctor] very voluntarily. And now he is personally giving me 130 pesos. Both my wife and I receive it in person before the witnesses. And the tribute will be remedied with [the price]; it will pay it. The land [upon which tribute is owed] is at Colonanco. It is adjacent to the land of

Altepetl: City-state.
Teopixqui: Priest, in Nahuatl.
Tlaxilacalli: Subunit of an *altepetl*.

Source: Rebecca Horn, "Spaniards in the Nahua Countryside: Dr. Diego de León Plaza and Nahuatl Land Sale Documents" (Mexico, Early Seventeenth Century), in Richard Boyer and Geoffrey Spurling, eds., *Colonial Lives: Documents on Latin American History, 1550–1850* (New York: Oxford University Press, 2000), 102–103, 108–109.

Miguel de Santiago and Lucas Pérez. And the witnesses [are] Antonio de Fuentes and señora Inés de Vera and Juana de Vera, Spanish women (and the Nahuas) Juan Josef, Gabriel Francisco, María, Mariana, and Sebastián Juan. And because we do not know how to write, I, Joaquín [de San] Francisco, and my wife asked a witness to set down [a signature] on our behalf [along with the notary?] Juan Vázquez, Spaniard. Witnesses, Antonio de Fuentes, [etc.] Before me, Matías Valeriano, notary. And both of them, he and his wife [Joaquín de San Francisco and Juana Feliciana], received the 140 pesos each three months, [presumably paid in installments?] before the witnesses who were mentioned. Before me, Matías Valeriano, notary.

. . .

[Letter of complaint to the authorities of Santo Domino Mixcoac, on the behalf of a group of Nahuas, undated:]

We are citizens here in Santo Domingo Mixcoac. We state that we found out that Paula and Juana and María and Catalina and Inés and Anastacia complain about the ***teniente*** before you [the *corregidor, gobernador, regidores,* etc.]. It is Antonio de Fuentes whom they are accusing because they say he mistreats them. [They say] he robs [people's land].

. . .

And now [the] Spaniard Napolles disputes with the *teniente*. And Napolles goes around to each house exerting pressure on, forcing many people [to say "get rid of the *teniente*"]. [He says:] "Let there be no officer of the justice. I will help you expel the *teniente* because we will be happy if there is no officer of the law on your land." Napolles, Spaniard, keeps a woman at his house and he is forcing her. For this reason [the authorities] arrested him for concubinage. They gave him a fine about which he became very angry and they arrested him. He stole four pigs, the property of a person named Francisco Hernández, Spaniard, and because of that they arrested him. He was scorched [burned] for their relatives accuse them.

. . .

And so now with great concern and with bowing down we implore you [the *corregidor, gobernador,* and *regidores,* etc.] and we ask for justice. Everyone knows how [the blacks and *mestizos*] mistreat us. They don't go to confession. They are already a little afraid and are already living a little better. And we ask for justice. Let them be punished. We who ask it are Juan Joseph, Francisco de San Juan, and Francisco Juan.

Teniente: Lieutenant.

WORKING WITH SOURCES

1. Why do the documents incorporate Nahuatl terms at some times but not at others?
2. How do the documents illustrate the various levels of justice available to native people and to "Spaniards"?

18.4 *The Jesuit Relations,* French North America, 1649

The Jesuit Relations are the most important documents attesting to the encounter between Europeans and native North Americans in the seventeenth century. These annual reports of French missionaries from the Society of Jesus document the conversions—or attempted conversions—of the various indigenous peoples in what is today the St. Lawrence River basin and the Great Lakes region.

Source: Paul Ragueneau, "Relation of 1648–49," in Allan Greer, ed., *The Jesuit Relations: Natives and Missionaries in Seventeenth-Century North America* (Boston: Bedford/St. Martin's, 2000), 112–115.

When they arrived on the banks of the St. Lawrence in 1625, French Jesuits were entering a continent still very much under control of First Nations peoples, who were divided by their own ethnic and linguistic differences. Even the catch-all terms "Huron" and "Iroquois" masked their nature as confederacies, composed of several distinct nations, who had joined together prior to the arrival of Europeans.

When the Jesuits made headway with one group, they usually lost initiative with the group's rivals—and sometimes found themselves in the midst of a conflict that they could barely understand or appreciate. This section of the *Relations* concerns the torture and murder of Jean Brébeuf, who had lived among the Hurons at various points from the 1620s through the 1640s, observing their culture and systematically attempting to convert them to Catholicism. However, when an Iroquois raiding party invaded his settlement, the depth of the Hurons' Christian commitment—and his own—would be tested.

The sixteenth day of March in the present year, 1649, marked the beginning of our misfortunes—if an event, which no doubt has been the salvation of many of God's elect, can be called a misfortune.

The Iroquois, enemies of the Hurons, arrived by night at the frontier of this country. They numbered about a thousand men, well furnished with weapons, most of them carrying firearms obtained from their allies, the Dutch. We had no knowledge of their approach, although they had started from their country in the autumn, hunting in the forests throughout the winter, and had made a difficult journey of nearly two hundred leagues over the snow in order to take us by surprise. By night, they reconnoitered the condition of the first place upon which they had designs. It was surrounded by a pine stockade fifteen or sixteen feet in height, and a deep ditch with which nature had strongly fortified this place on three sides. There remained only a small space that was weaker than the others.

It was at this weak point that the enemy made a breach at daybreak, but so secretly and promptly that he was master of the place before anyone could mount a defense. All were then sleeping deeply, and they had no time to recognize the danger. Thus this village was taken, almost without striking a blow and with only ten Iroquois killed. Part of the Hurons—men, women, and children—were massacred then and there, while the others were made captives and were reserved for cruelties more terrible than death.

. . .

The enemy did not stop there, but followed up his victory, and before sunrise he appeared in arms to attack the town of St. Louis, which was fortified with a fairly good stockade. Most of the women and the children had just gone from it upon hearing the news which had arrived regarding the approach of the Iroquois. The people of greatest courage, about eighty persons, being resolved to defend themselves well, courageously repulsed the first and the second assaults, killing about thirty of the enemy's boldest men, in addition to many wounded. But finally, the larger number prevailed, as the Iroquois used their hatchets to undermine the palisade of stakes and opened a passage for themselves through some considerable breaches.

About nine o'clock in the morning, we perceived from our house at St. Marie the fire which was consuming the cabins of that town, where the enemy, after entering victoriously, had reduced everything to desolation. They cast into the flames the old, the sick, the children who had not been able to escape, and all those who, being too severely wounded, could not have followed them into captivity. At the sight of those flames, and by the color of the smoke which issued from them, we understood sufficiently what was happening, for this town of St. Louis was no more than a league distant from us. Two Christians who escaped the fire arrived about this time and confirmed this.

In this town of St. Louis were at that time two of our fathers, Father Jean de Brébeuf and Father Gabriel

Lalemant, who had charge of a cluster of five towns. These formed but one of the eleven missions of which we have spoken above, and we call it the mission of St. Ignace.

Some Christians had begged the fathers to preserve their lives for the glory of God, which would have been as easy for them as for the more than five hundred persons who went away at the first alarm, for there was more than enough time to reach a place of safety. But their zeal could not permit such a thing, and the salvation of their flock was dearer to them than the love of their own lives. They employed the moments left to them as the most precious which they had ever had in the world, and through the heat of the battle their hearts were on fire for the salvation of souls. One was at the breach, baptizing the **catechumens**, and the other was giving absolution to the **neophytes**. Both of them urged the Christians to die in the sentiments of piety with which they consoled them in their miseries. Never was their faith more alive, nor their love for their good fathers and pastors more keenly felt.

An infidel, seeing the desperate situation, spoke of taking flight, but a Christian named Etienne Annaotaha, the most esteemed in the country for his courage and his exploits against the enemy, would never allow it. "What!" he said. "Could we ever abandon these two good fathers, who have exposed their lives for us? Their love for our salvation will be the cause of their death, for there is no longer time for them to flee across the snows. Let us then die with them, and we shall go together to heaven." This man had made a general confession a few days previously, having had a presentiment of the danger awaiting him and saying that he wished that death should find him disposed for Heaven. And indeed he, as well as many other Christians, had abandoned themselves to fervor in a manner so extraordinary that we shall never be sufficiently able to bless the guidance of God over so many predestinated souls. His divine providence continues lovingly to guide them in death as in life.

Catechumens: Native converts who had not yet been baptized.
Neophytes: Recently baptized Christians.

WORKING WITH SOURCES

1. How well do the Jesuits seem to have understood the conflicts among native peoples in this region?
2. How was Ragueneau's reporting of the battle designed to highlight the "success" of the mission, despite an apparent setback?

18.5 The Salem Witch Trials, British North America, 1692

The witch hunt that took place in Salem, Massachusetts, in 1692 has been frequently (if sensationally) depicted in modern films and plays. But a reading of the extant documents used in the trial of the supposed witches provides a more nuanced insight into the process of denunciation, conviction, and execution that unfolded in this persecution, which was among the last in the Western world. Although the Salem witch hunt resulted in the conviction of 30 and the execution of 19, the total number of persons who had been formally accused reached 164. Doubts about the guilt of those executed eventually led to a reconsideration of the procedures used in the trial, and the governor of the colony abruptly suspended the trials in the autumn of 1692. In spite of the admission by some of the Salem jurors that they had been mistaken, the judgments passed on seven of the convicted were not reversed until 2001.

Source: Brian P. Levack, ed., *The Witchcraft Sourcebook* (New York: Routledge, 2004), 225–226, 228–229.

Samuel Gray of Salem, aged about 42 years, testifieth and saith that about fourteen years ago, he going to bed well one [a.m.] one Lord's Day at night, and after he had been asleep some time, he awakened and looking up, saw the house light as if a candle or candles were lighted in it and the door locked, and that little fire there was raked up. He did then see a woman standing between the cradle in the room and the bedside and seemed to look upon him. So he did rise up in his bed and it vanished or disappeared. Then he went to the door and found it locked, and unlocking and opening the door, he went to the entry door and looked out and then again did see the same woman he had a little before seen in the room and in the same garb she was in before. Then he said to her, "What in the name of God do you come for?" Then she vanished away, so he locked the door again and went to bed, and between sleeping and waking he felt something come to his mouth or lips cold, and thereupon started and looked up again and did see the same woman with some thing between both her hands holding before his mouth upon which she moved. And the child in the cradle gave a great screech out as if it was greatly hurt and she disappeared, and taking the child up could not quiet it in some hours from which time the child that was before a very lively, thriving child did pine away and was never well, although it lived some months after, yet in a sad condition and so died. Some time after within a week or less he did see the same woman in the same garb and clothes that appeared to him as aforesaid, and although he knew not her nor her name before, yet both by the countenance and garb doth testify that it was the same woman that they now call Bridget Bishop, alias Oliver, of Salem. Sworn Salem, May 30th 1692.

. . .

The deposition of Joseph Ring at Salisbury, aged 27 years, being sworn, saith that about the latter end of September last, being in the wood with his brother Jarvis Ring hewing of timber, his brother went home with his team and left this deponent alone to finish the hewing of the piece for him for his brother to carry when he came again. But as soon as his brother was gone there came to this deponent the appearance of Thomas Hardy of the great island of Puscataway, and by some impulse he was forced to follow him to the house of Benovy Tucker, which was deserted and about a half a mile from the place he was at work in, and in that house did appear Susannah Martin of Amesbury and the aforesaid Hardy and another female person which the deponent did not know. There they had a good fire and drink—it seemed to be cider. There continued most part of the night, [the] said Martin being then in her natural shape and talking as if she used to. But towards the morning the said Martin went from the fire, made a noise, and turned into the shape of a black hog and went away, and so did the other. Two persons go away, and this deponent was strangely carried away also, and the first place he knew was by Samuel Woods' house in Amesbury.

. . .

The deposition of Thomas Putnam, aged 40 years and [Edward Putnam] aged 38 years, who testify and say that we have been conversant with the afflicted persons or the most of them, as namely Mary Walcott, Mercy Lewes, Elizabeth Hubbard, Abigail Williams, Sarah Bibber and Ann Putnam junior and have often heard the aforementioned persons complain of Susannah Martin of Amesbery [sic] torturing them, and we have seen the marks of several bites and pinches which they say Susannah Martin did hurt them with, and also on the second day of May 1692, being the day of the examination of Susannah Martin, the aforenamed persons were most grievously tortured during the time of her examination, for upon a glance of her eyes they were struck down or almost choked and upon the motion of her finger we took notes they were afflicted, and if she did but clench her hands or hold her head aside the afflicted persons aforementioned were most grievously tortured, complaining of Susannah Martin for hurting them.

WORKING WITH SOURCES

1. What do these documents suggest about the (supposed) powers of witches, especially in terms of acting at a distance upon their victims?
2. Although all of the witnesses in this set of documents were men, do they reveal something about the connection between witchcraft accusations and gender?